At Home in the Dark

At Home in the Dark

Conversations with Ten American Poets

David Elliott

Keystone College Press
La Plume, Pennsylvania

Keystone College Press
Keystone College
One College Green
La Plume, PA 18440

www.keystone.edu

First Edition

Set in Calibri

Layout and Design by Raymond P. Hammond

Cover Photograph by David Elliott

Author Photo by Carolyn Elliott

Keystone College Press Logo by Ashley Purdy, Class of 2018

Work Study / Editorial Assistant: Aleigh Smith, Class of 2019

Proof Editing by Kimberly Boland, Class of 2017

Library of Congress Control Number: 2018943776

ISBN: 978-1-64042-500-2 (Hardback Edition)

          978-1-64042-501-9 (Paperback Edition)

At Home in the Dark

Conversations with Ten American Poets

CONTENTS

Preface / ix

I. Language Is the Articulation of Myth / 3
A Conversation with W. S. Merwin

II. At Home in the Dark / 31
A Conversation with William Stafford

III. Tracking the Mind / 57
A Conversation with Robert Creeley

IV. A Struggle Between Silence and Words / 79
A Conversation with David Ray

V. The Surprise of Writing / 91
A Conversation with Robert Morgan

VI. Home Keeps Getting Bigger / 111
A Conversation with Naomi Shihab Nye

VII. Precarious Balances / 123
A Conversation with Stephen Dunn

VIII. Finding a Distinctive Voice / 141
A Conversation with Lucien Stryk

IX. Praise Is a Generative Act / 161
A Conversation with Pattiann Rogers

X. The Complexity of the Human Heart / 179
A Conversation with Marie Howe

Acknowledgments / 195

Preface

These conversations took place over a sixteen-year period starting in 1984. They were the result of my being involved in the organization of two poetry reading series, one in the city of Scranton, Pennsylvania, and one at Keystone College in nearby La Plume. As seasons were planned and upcoming readings approached, I knew there were certain poets with whom I hoped to talk at length, poets whom I was particularly interested in and whose work I wanted to explore with them in conversation. Sometimes it was possible, but more often not, what with the usual routine of events before and after the readings. But it was not until several years had passed that I decided to pursue these conversations with some of the poets at length and more formally for publication. I made the arrangements to set aside the time, and in most cases the conversations took place the day of the readings.

The poets I spoke with were not representative of a single school or style of contemporary American poetry. Similarly, what I wanted to talk about differed from poet to poet. I did not have an overall program, a particular angle I wanted to pursue in all the interviews. Rather, each poet's work raised specific issues I wanted him or her to discuss, so the conversations vary in focus. However, there were some issues—the musicality of poetry, the process of writing, the relationship between the poetry and the life of the poet—that were discussed by more than one poet. With all of the conversations now collected together in this book, these common issues sometimes create a kind of crosstalk between the poets.

The first conversation, with W. S. Merwin, took place a year after his appearance in Scranton, when I proposed to him the idea of doing one. His schedule was full and he was living in Hawaii, so it was not until October 1984 that I traveled to New York City to visit him in the Greenwich Village apartment he had kept for years. He was only spending three weeks in New York that year, and two or three days after the interview he was to return to Maui. Much of our wide-ranging conversation was focused on myth, its relation to his poetry and to what was then referred to as deep imagery. We concluded with a discussion of his environmental concerns and his recent writing projects, especially his interest in the natural and human history of Hawaii, which ultimately led to his 1998 book-length poem *The Folding Cliffs*.

William Stafford read at Keystone College in March 1988. In our conversation later that afternoon, Stafford talked at length about a variety of topics with his characteristically plainspoken humility. He had so much to say that our conversation continued in the car as I drove him to the airport with the tape recorder on the dashboard. The route I took involved turning onto a highway that reversed direction for a short while. In mid-answer, Stafford briefly stopped talking and asked if I was sure I was going the right way. I was, but it was in the way his answers often did, somewhat circuitously. Much of our conversation involved poetry, of course, but we covered so many issues that the material was edited into three versions, with some overlap, that were published separately. The first and longest version was primarily literary in focus, the second dealt with his religious life and pacifism, and the third explored his ideas on the teaching of writing.

One month later I spoke with Robert Creeley in his Scranton hotel room on the afternoon of his reading in April 1988. I knew we shared an interest in jazz, and so I wanted him to talk about his experiences listening to the music and about its influence on his poetry, primarily in terms of improvisation and rhythm. He reminisced about hearing Charlie Parker, John Coltrane, Thelonious Monk, Ornette Coleman, and others. We also discussed two jazz recordings in which Steve Swallow and Steve Lacy set his poems to music and whether they captured the rhythmic feel of his poems and his characteristic line breaks. Listening to Creeley during our conversation, with his starts and stops, his pivots from one point to another, was like listening to one of his poems extended for an hour or so.

David Ray read his poetry in April 1991 during the Kurdish Uprising, two months after the cease-fire that concluded Operation Desert Storm, the first Gulf War. The history of those days weighed heavily in our conversation, which took place in a church in downtown Scranton. A co-founder with Robert Bly of the American Writers Against the Vietnam War, Ray has had a long history of social and political activism. He had also taught abroad in several countries, including India, and he spoke of his experiences there, which he had written about in *The Maharani's New Wall,* his most recent book of poetry at that time.

Robert Morgan was interviewed in January 1992, a few months after his reading in Scranton. I traveled to his home on the outskirts of

Ithaca, New York, on a sunny Saturday afternoon. His *Green River: New and Selected Poems* had just been published, and we talked about his entire writing career, which was put into perspective when he assembled that book. A transplanted Southerner, he spoke about the use of subject matter from his North Carolina heritage. Versification, free verse, and formalism provided other areas of discussion.

In March of 1992, Naomi Shihab Nye attended a reading by Hayden Carruth at Keystone College prior to her reading in Scranton that evening. In between these two events she and I were able to have our conversation in the Faculty Lounge of the college's library. We began by talking about the importance of storytelling in her poetry, as well as the role of personal memory. Both of these concerns were discussed in light of Nye's bicultural heritage as the daughter of an American mother and a Palestinian father. Her feelings about the role of poetry in people's lives were also on her mind as we talked.

Stephen Dunn read at Keystone College in March of 1993, and following the reading our conversation also took place in the college's library. We talked about craft issues—the music and rhythms of sentences and lines, as well as narrative point of view. He also had put together a volume of new and selected poems and talked about his choices of what to include. Reference was made to his basketball career in college and then as a semi-pro player for nearby Williamsport, Pennsylvania, and he discussed parallels between playing basketball and writing poetry. The conversation concluded with time enough to watch a televised NCAA tournament game.

Although Lucien Stryk published many books of his own poetry and was primarily reading from those books when he appeared in Scranton in April 1994, my conversation with him on that day was primarily about Japanese haiku poetry and his translations of classic poets like Basho and Issa. As a haiku poet, I was interested in speaking with him about the challenges of translating poetry and about what makes haiku a particular challenge. He did not himself write haiku, but he did discuss the influence of haiku on his own poetry and how some of his poems can be seen as having haiku-like passages.

Pattiann Rogers visited Scranton in November 1995. Her poetry interested me largely because of the way it incorporates a knowledge of science, especially biology. I had considered majoring in biology in college but, like, Rogers decided on an English major. This gave us a lot to talk about in our conversation, including the topic of language with regard to how it is used in science and whether that uasge can be successfully incorporated into poetry, as well as the issue of how language affects perception. She also discussed her relation to nature writing.

The final conversation, with Marie Howe, took place following her reading at Keystone College in May 2000. She spoke of the importance of moments of transformation both in her life and her poetry, recalling how she had left high school teaching to pursue her life as a poet. Although her second book, *What the Living Do*, dealt largely with the death of her brother from AIDS, she said that the concept of confessional poetry and the personal narrative was problematic for her. She also reflected on what keeps poetry alive as an art and its role in contemporary society. Appropriately for the end of this book, she concluded with an assertion of her faith in poetry even in a time that seems to devalue authentic language.

David Elliott
June 2018

At Home in the Dark

Conversations with Ten American Poets

I. Language Is the Articulation of Myth

A Conversation with W. S. Merwin

Greenwich Village, New York, New York
October 1984

W. S. Merwin (b. 1927) was twice a winner of the Pulitzer Prize (for *The Carrier of Ladders* and *The Shadow of Sirius*) and was named the Poet Laureate of the United States in 2010. In addition to his poetry, he published volumes of translations, prose, and plays.

ELLIOTT: I'd like to start with a brief excerpt from Auden's foreword to your first book, *A Mask for Janus*, where he talks about your "concern for the traditional conceptions of Western culture as expressed in its myths" [ix]. Did you agree with that statement then, and whether you did then or not, do you now think it an accurate assessment of your very earliest career, with the emphasis on Western?

MERWIN: Auden was pointing out something that I hadn't thought of as a program, obviously, and I would agree with it now, but my notion of what it means would be very different from what I thought it meant when I was in my early career. I now think that myth is something like the intuition of a kind of coherent sense of experience, which we can't live without. But it is our own projection. It is real in the sense that it's necessary. To us.

ELLIOTT: Was there then a shift from thinking of myth as something borrowed, something received or transmitted from a past culture, to a sense of the mythic consciousness in one's own mind, which is capable of creating modern myth?

MERWIN: Yes. I think that any real use of language is mythic in some sense. Language is myth. Language is articulation of myth.

ELLIOTT: Did any of the change in your attitude toward myth come from exploring primitive mythology through some of the poetry you were translating?

MERWIN: I'm sure it did, but I'm sure that everything contributed to it, and to thinking I had had enough to do with myth and wanted to look in other directions, realizing that mythology really informed everything, that mythology was not merely something you learned in school that the Greeks had to make statues to illustrate a couple of thousand years ago. It is everything that helps us to make sense of the world.

ELLIOTT: Did you come to feel that, for all of its perceptiveness in many realms of life, Greek myth was becoming somehow inadequate as a means of coming to terms with certain problems of contemporary civilization, such as the possible extinction of nature or the extinction of man?

MERWIN: Maybe. But I think that all of the mythologies come from a place that is so deep that they really do deal with experiences very remote from their original statements. For a long time, for example, it seemed to me that the myths of Phaethon and Orpheus were complementary ways of looking at two different attitudes toward the world that we still find around us. One is the Orphic one, which evokes a harmonious relation with the whole living world. And the myth of Phaethon, of course, is a myth based on ego, envy, and exploitation, in which you try to take the chariot into the sun and drive it whether you can drive it or not, and you end up by destroying what you drive over and being destroyed yourself.

ELLIOTT: Was there a point at which oriental myth became important to you in a way that it hadn't been before?

MERWIN: Gradually, yes.

ELLIOTT: Is there a sense in which Buddhism and Zen require a different attitude toward myth from the traditional Western attitude? People are fond of making distinctions between the Eastern mind and the Western mind, sometimes too facilely, but do you find a different approach to myth in Buddhism?

MERWIN: Oh, it's certainly different. I'd be shy of trying to describe the difference. And, of course, myths are used differently in different traditions of Buddhism, particularly Mahayana. In Theravada, the main myth is the myth of the historic Buddha, whatever we know of the historic Buddha. Mahayana Buddhism is highly mythological but also highly abstract. On the other hand, some of the koans that are used in Zen are myth, are folktales.

ELLIOTT: I'd like to read a passage from your foreword to Robert Aitken's *A Zen Wave:*

> there has been no presentation of Basho's work, and the experience of which it is a manifestation, in terms of the particular cast of Basho's religious insight into his world and ours. To underestimate this aspect of Basho's writing and his life is to risk missing what he himself evidently took to be the center of them both, the essence of his nature and his art, and the secret of the relation between them. (11)

6

Do you feel that the same statement can now or could from the start be made about your poetry?

MERWIN: I don't think it could have been made at the beginning. I'm not even sure it could be now. I think the danger of a statement like that is a sort of sectarian interpretation, so that you have to understand the kind of ideology that the poems are coming from before you can really understand them. Dogen, for example, refused to call Zen *Zen*. I mean he called Zen *Zen*, but he kept saylng, "We must not even think of this as Buddhism. It is the awakened way that we are talking about. We're talking about being awake." And I think this is really the link between that kind of experience and the poetry of Basho or any real poetry that is not simply decorative. One is trying to project and articulate an insight about experience itself—about the experience of being.

ELLIOTT: But is the demonstration or assertion of the importance of an awakened vision something you would take now to be central to your work?

MERWIN: Yes. I mean I'm trying to make sense of things. It is very easy to get drawn off into a metaphysical discussion of it, which I don't think is much help, and I wouldn't want to convey the impression at all that I thought that in order to understand anybody's poems, including mine, one had to have a particular point of view. I don't think, for example, this is true of Dante. One doesn't have to be a Catholic for *The Divine Comedy* to go on informing one's life. One doesn't need to get any closer to orthodox Christianity for that to be so, or I don't believe that one does. I feel great obligation and gratitude to Dante, and I am not a Christian.

ELLIOTT: I understand your point. It would be entirely possible for somebody to read your work and not have any idea that Buddhism was an interest of yours, and yet an understanding of Buddhism indicates that there are some parallels or influence there.

MERWIN: But I think that it is there in many bodies of poetry where I, at least, wasn't aware of it. For example, although it didn't occur to me at the time I was translating him, there is something of that same insight in the work of Jean Follain. Whether it had any sectarian nourishment or not, I don't know—he had a certain amount to do with Trappist contemplatives.

But I think it is far more common than one is led to expect. That is one of the disadvantages of making this easy distinction between East and West and then waving a flag over one of them. I mean any time in any of the arts—and after all, this is almost the condition of an art—that you make the absolutely specific and unique instance of something a representative of *everything*, you're giving voice to that insight, and it doesn't matter whether you do it from a Christian point of view or from a supposedly atheist point of view or from a Buddhist point of view or a Hindu point of view. It really doesn't matter.

ELLIOTT: In the poems of *The Moving Target, The Lice,* and *The Carrier of Ladders,* there seems to be the expression of much suffering—both personal suffering, in statements like "my mind is divided" and so on, and also, of course, cultural, political, and ecological suffering, the suffering of nature. I'm wondering if that was an expression of the frame of mind that was leading you to an interest in Buddhism.

MERWIN: Probably, yes. I think it was certainly all part of the same movement. There were personal things that had to do with finding my way through some years that involved quite a number of decisions. I mean some quite obvious ones involving New York and living in the city or the country, but also with regard to America, the alien past and present. And certainly, most of *The Lice* was written at a time when I really felt there was no point in writing. I got to the point where I thought the future so bleak that there was no point in writing anything at all. And so the poems kind of pushed their way upon me when I wasn't thinking of writing. I would be out growing vegetables and walking around the countryside when all of a sudden I'd find myself writing a poem, and I'd write it, and that was the way most of *The Lice* was written.

ELLIOTT: It seems to have been a prolific time in your life in terms of poetic output.

MERWIN: It did happen rather fast, yes. A lot of *The Lice* was written in a couple of years. I don't feel much more optimistic about the historic aspect of our experience than I did then, but people have been saying how the more recent poetry seems more calm. I feel, I suppose, that the place of saying something is a little bit different from what I thought it was then. We're born and we very soon know that we are going to die.

That's not a reason not to live with it, however. But the feeling of distress and anger and grief that is there in *The Lice* is there really through all of the poems. I don't know of any way of shrugging it off. I don't see that our culture and our species are behaving in a more enlightened and gentle and harmonious fashion now than we were twenty years ago. And the cause of the anger is, I suppose, the feeling of destruction, watching the destruction of things that I care passionately about. If we're so stupid that we choose to destroy each other and ourselves, that's bad enough; but if we destroy the whole life on the planet! And I'm not talking about a big bang; I'm talking about something that is happening as we are sitting here talking about it—the destruction of seas, the destruction of species after species, the destruction of the forests. These are not replaceable. We can't suddenly decide years down the line that we made a mistake and put it all back. The feeling of awe—something that we seem to be losing—is essential for survival.

ELLIOTT: Is the overcoming of your feeling that writing was not to the point or impossible related in any way to that Buddhist paradox: because something is impossible and because you acknowledge that it is impossible, you are thereby enabled to try to do it anyway?

MERWIN: It's always impossible in some place. I mean poetry is impossible, speech is impossible, life is probably impossible, but we go on living. The bee can't fly, but it doesn't know it, so it flies happily along. An easier way to say something about it is to evoke a passage from Thoreau. Somewhere in the journals, he is talking with grief about the enclosure of the Concord Common, and he says, people won't be able to let their animals roam as they please, and won't be able to pick huckleberries. It will no longer be a free place. It will belong to somebody. And he is very eloquent, as he always is about that. But then he says the other thing. He says, I was not sufficiently aware of it; I didn't pay enough attention; I didn't love it hard enough when I had it. I think it is possible to pay so much attention to how angry we are that we forget why we are angry; and if we are angry for any reason except because we want to save things that we love and can't to pay attention to the fact that we do love them, then we've helped to destroy ourselves at the root.

ELLIOTT: So is it a matter of becoming nonattached to anger? Do you feel that in the sixties anger became so much an end in itself that it was counterproductive and not pushing something forward that might have helped the problems you were so concerned about?

MERWIN: You always are a little frustrated. The part of you that writes poems hoping that it will make something happen, which is the part of you that's writing propaganda, is always there. Poetry isn't so pure that it's completely devoid of that. You wouldn't want it to be. Pure poetry is an antimacassar, isn't it? It's a decoration. You do want something to happen, even if it is only to get somebody to move something. When we wrote poems during the Vietnam war we wanted the poems to stop the war. When you write a poem out of grief, what do you want? We still don't know, but we are trying to complete something that we feel is incomplete.

ELLIOTT: I would like to stay with that period of the sixties for a little while. Does the term "deep image" have any meaning for you?

MERWIN: I can remember when Jerry Rothenberg and Jerry's friends talked a lot about deep image back in the early sixties and late fifties. It means something in a historical sense. But I always thought they were loading the term unnecessarily. I thought that what they were really talking about was an image that came from where all real images come from, which is not out of the footnotes or wholly out of the promptings of other poems, but out of the oddities and uniqueness of one's own experiences. A real image always comes from that singular "deep" place, dripping with surprise. Coleridge talked about the difference between fancy and imagination, and I think what Coleridge meant by imagination was pretty much what Jerry meant by deep image, where the disparate becomes *one*—the apparently disparate is seen as a whole. There is a real moment of fusion, of heat, and of urgency involved.

ELLIOTT: For better or worse, at that time the term seemed to gather into it the connotations of a quasi surrealism.

MERWIN: Yes, that always bothered me a little. I mean I have never been as fond of surrealism as some people were in the sixties. I think surrealism was absolutely essential to read and pay attention to, but it's a place I never wanted to get stuck in. To me, almost all surrealism tends to become very two-dimensional. Some depth missing.

ELLIOTT: There often tends to be a kind of arbitrariness about surrealism.

MERWIN: The very thing it says it's avoiding. It used to make me impatient to be called a surrealistic poet. When many critics don't understand how metaphor works, they decide that it's surrealistic.

ELLIOTT: It's almost as if calling it surrealist gives you license to ignore it.

MERWIN: Yes. It's a way of shrugging it off by putting it in its category: we know about surrealism, so that takes care of that. I think a lot of imagery that seems very clear to readers is so because it is familiar, and it is familiar because it is doing something that has already been done, and any new use of imagery sets up resistances and defenses which make it seem incomprehensible, whereas fifteen years later it will look perfectly simple. One of the things that always used to give me heart when I was described as hopelessly obscure and surrealist was that children were not having any trouble at all reading the poems.

Another reason I think this is happening is because we are living in a more and more artificial world. We are living in a world surrounded by human contraptions instead of living creatures, and I profoundly believe this is something that can't go on. I don't think we can live in a completely human-made world. The imagery continues to come out of the place that requires something beyond human fabrication, beyond human origin of things. And this, I think, is why even people who don't live all the time in the country, if they are above a certain age, will tend to use imagery that has to do with the natural world, and more and more readers can't understand it.

I remember when Robert Bly came to visit me in France years ago. He was talking about surrealism in my poems and mentioned an image about a fly turning around a statue of nothing and said it was surrealistic. And I said, "It's *not*, Robert," and I took him into a room on the farm and showed him flies going round and round and round in a circle, in the middle of the room.

I can't imagine being able to live without the natural world. I wouldn't want to live in a world that was completely fabricated. It seems to me to be completely out of touch with what I think of as real, which involves the mystery of other forms of life. We need them; I certainly do. I think our destruction of other species is disastrous to our own minds.

ELLIOTT: But despite your feeling that labeling your poetry as surrealist was really not to the point, nonetheless there was a period during which many of the images in your poems seem truly anomalous in the same was as surrealism can be, and recently that's much less the case.

MERWIN: Well, there definitely were poems, particularly some of the first poems in *The Lice*, that were a deliberate attempt to use certain surrealist devices to convey the same kind of things the other poems were conveying in other ways. Those really might have been called surrealist, but they were seldom the ones that were talked about. For example, "The Unfinished Book of Kings." But even that poem depends on the kind of dramatic coherence which surrealism very often tries to do without.

ELLIOTT: Much surrealism is very static.

MERWIN: Yes.

ELLIOTT: Is that the reason why you've left that kind of poem behind?

MERWIN: Well, when you've written something, you don't have to write it again. That's reason enough to leave it behind.

ELLIOTT: The feeling that I get from your poetry in the sixties, and which is something that many people have said about your poetry then, is that it gives the feeling of a world stripped down to essences. Is there a connection between the anger and despair you were experiencing and your use at that time of a kind of imagery that does not look on the page as if it is giving a detailed vision of the phenomenal world, as much of your later poetry does? Is that shift from the imagery in *The Lice* to the imagery of later poetry in some way connected with overcoming or coming to terms with the anger and bitterness and maybe dealing more closely with the things in the world?

MERWIN: I wanted to accept more and more aspects of the world. Certain things are no more acceptable than ever, of course; but wanting to be more intimate and closer to things and to be able to take the real day-to-day details of existence and use them, and to have that kind of closeness—that's been the real intent.

ELLIOTT: During that time in the sixties to early seventies some of the images could be characterized as being dark in a negative sense, using a word like "emptiness" with negative connotations of the void in a way that might express a kind of existential dread. And yet there is the Buddhist concept of emptiness which is really a kind of fullness. I am wondering whether the negative emptiness—the way that many Westerners think of the world as empty—seemed to be more appropriate at that time, but now it's emptiness in the sense of fullness that you are interested in.

MERWIN: Yes, I think that is probably true. Although I have to keep saying that I don't feel historically much more optimistic.

ELLIOTT: Have you ever thought that in the period of *The Lice*, when your poetry often seemed stripped down and there was much use of silence and space, the interplay between the words and the surrounding space was somewhat like sumi painting? I sometimes get the same feel out of those poems, as if they were just a few brush strokes and not concerned with photographic detail.

MERWIN: I wouldn't have made the analogy, but I see what you mean. I really wanted something that was utterly compressed. You know, something that was portable, something you could take with you—and that you might want to take with you.

ELLIOTT: How do you feel about the poems of that period now? Are you somewhat distanced from them? They seem so different from the poems of the past few years.

MERWIN: I couldn't write them now. I *wouldn't* write them now, but I don't feel so distant. No. They are all part of a story, and there is no point in trying to erase parts of the story. You can't do it. That was twenty-five years ago almost. So I do feel *that* distance from them. On the other hand, they were a breakthrough into a place which was a perfectly authentic place for me. I had to write them.

ELLIOTT: Looking back, do you feel that possibly you were keeping the world at a greater distance—holding back from it because of the negative things that you saw—and that that was somehow done more compatibly in a poetry that erased the particulars?

13

MERWIN: You know the old problem: if you simply string together a whole lot of particulars, it is not a poem. Particulars do what surrealist images do. They become two-dimensional and there is no shape to the whole thing. There is no reason. It becomes like reading a telephone book.

ELLIOTT: Was the poetry of that period valuable to you partly because of what you were learning about form?

MERWIN: About what made a poem have a certain kind of life to it, let's say, and vibrancy, which seemed to me essential, and I would happily have incorporated as many particulars as possible, but just incorporating particulars wasn't going to make it happen.

ELLIOTT: You rarely wrote poems at that point like "Green Water Tower" or "The Sea Cliffs at Kailua in December," for example, in your recent book *Opening the Hand*, where it seems as if they are describing specific places that you are familiar with. Not that you are describing them in great photographic detail, but they seem like real places, whereas so many of the poems in *The Lice* seem as if they could be anywhere.

MERWIN: Most of them were about real places. They present a perception about a real place. It wasn't a matter of withholding detail; it was a matter of trying to do something else with the experience. The particulars were not so much the things that seemed to convey it as was some kind of perception about the experience of a place itself, of being there. At least that's how I thought of it then—and don't now.

ELLIOTT: Another way of pointing to a difference between your poetry in the sixties and early seventies and the more recent poetry has to do with the voice. In the same way that the particularity of the world is more present in the recent poetry, so the particularity of the speaker seems more evident in the recent poems. And in your foreword to *A Zen Wave*, in talking about Basho, you refer to "the profound intimacy of this poetry into which the postures and qualifications and noise of an 'I' obtrude relatively so little" [Aitken 15]. With regard to your own poetry, that statement is no less true of your more recent work than it was for the poetry at the time of *The Lice*, and yet at the same time it seems as if the real historical figure, the writer behind the poem, was somehow again at greater remove in the earlier period.

MERWIN: Yes.

ELLIOTT: From what came that act of putting yourself into the forefront of the poem a little bit more?

MERWIN: I suppose being able to accept some more things. I couldn't even say what they are. I don't know what they are. It would be very easy to say "accepting oneself," which of course is part of it. But it's something that I always wanted. You can't often write the poems you want to write. You write what you can, and you write closer to things sometimes—often with a sense of surprise.

ELLIOTT: In your career, as with so many other poets there for a long while, were you quite consciously influenced by Eliot's ideas on the impersonal nature of poetry?

MERWIN: He was so much around it would have been very hard not to be. He seemed to be present the way Freud would be present if you were talking about psychology.

ELLIOTT: Then there were reactions against that influence in so many different directions: the confessional poets, the Beats, for example. But one of the things that seemed to be the case with your poetry was that instead of going from the Eliot-influenced impersonal to the very narrowly personal, as some poets did, it was as if the voice in those poems, from *The Moving Target* on, became somehow transpersonal; or if it was going from the objective to the subjective, it was quite radically subjective, so that some people would mistake it for objectivity when in truth it was not. Does that seem to tally with your sense of what you were doing then?

MERWIN: Yes. But you know when I say anything about that, it is hindsight, because there wasn't at any point a calculated program of what to do next. I mean with some poets, Bly, for example, there probably was, and with Denise Levertov there certainly was. But I never sat down and thought, "Well, now I should do this, now I should do that, now I should do something else." I finished the poems in *The Drunk in the Furnace*, and I didn't know where I was going next. I knew I wasn't going to do the same thing over again.

ELLIOTT: Toward the end of that book you included those family portraits which seemed to be bringing the autobiographical self into the poem more, and then you left them behind, as if that kind of narrowly personal poetry was somehow not what was needed.

MERWIN: I felt that I could come to depend on what could be described as a subject matter, and be stuck, and be defined, and define myself by it and feel that I couldn't do anything else. That's very easy to do.

ELLIOTT: And then twenty years later you come back and write about some of the same relatives, in *Unframed Originals*, which is unabashedly factual, or at least it appears that way, and also in *Opening the Hand*. But perhaps because of having gone through that phase of *The Lice* it seems now as if the poems in which you are dealing with your family are much more effectively personal than those in *The Drunk in the Furnace*.

MERWIN: Just with age, if you are lucky, you may learn how to make that happen. The earlier poems seem to be more distant than what I write now. I wouldn't like to write from such a distance. I made little attempts to write autobiographical things in my twenties and early thirties. I put them all aside. One talks about perspective, which really implies distance from things, but actually one has to arrive at a certain perspective before one really can be intimate about them. Usually, the first autobiographical novel is just a way of getting the arm warmed up for being able to write something else, and later on the writer will come back to that material and be able to do something with it.

ELLIOTT: One of the many associations with the title of *Opening the Hand*, in addition to suggesting the poem about your parents' hands, is that it seems a gesture of acceptance to me, a kind of acceptance of the world. I think of the difference in tone between "The Coming Extinction" and "The Shore." They are essentially about the same subject. And yet the more recent poem seems much more tender. There's certainly no more of an acceptance of the horrible conditions that are creating these ecological changes, but it's as if you and the whale are are on more intimate grounds with each other, in terms of the language of the poem, than in the earlier poem, which didn't seem to have so much of a connection with the creature itself.

MERWIN: I hope that is true. There is no difference between us and the whales in the last poem.

16

ELLIOTT: As I was going back through *Writings to an Unfinished Accompaniment*, I noticed more clearly than I had before how many poems are dealing with eyes and vision. It seems to be quite a strong, recurring theme. That sent me back to a stanza in "Words from a Totem Animal": "My eyes are waiting for me / in the dusk / they are still closed / they have been waiting a long time / and I am feeling my way toward them" [Carrier 16]. There is an interesting progression in *Writings* where the achievement of vision and of eyes capable of seeing seems to be more and more possible. And then there's the poem "The Initiate," which goes one step further to say that we don't even need the eyes, implying an inward vision. But *Writings* seems to represent a transitional period in your poetry from the three books that preceded it, and most of the poems in that book, to what happens in the poetry in *The Compass Flower, Finding the Islands*, and *Opening the Hand*, where all of a sudden it is as if the world is let in more freely, is seen with great particularity.

MERWIN: That's interesting. I never thought of that, but you may very well be right. It certainly was a time of trying to see and find a way through to just what you have been describing. Whether it worked or not I never thought to look back and see. I never know what the next poem will be. I never know if there is going to be a next poem.

ELLIOTT: Is there a historical referent to "Finding a Teacher" in terms of your own experience? That poem from *Writings* seems like a little Zen parable.

MERWIN: No, there isn't. It wasn't that way at all. That was before I'd ever found any kind of Zen teacher. I'd always imagined that a teacher would be an animal. I still think that's true. I think animals really are our teachers in many essentials.

ELLIOTT: But to return to the change in your poetry, in relation to the poems of *The Compass Flower*, it is almost as if those three earlier books, from *The Moving Target* on, were, in anthropological terms, a kind of initiation experience, like a going out into the barren wilderness. There is so much that seems negative in them. Do *The Compass Flower, Finding the Islands,* and *Opening the Hand* feel of a piece to you, in the way that *The Moving Target, The Lice,* and *The Carrier of Ladders* are?

MERWIN: I suppose so. *Opening the Hand*, to me, seems to be separate from the two others.

ELLIOTT: I was going to ask that. But it does seem informed by the kind of more detailed perception of the world that those previous two books have. The poems in *Finding the Islands* even resemble haiku in their attention to the details of particular moments. But I have heard you read from that book and you were very careful to say, "these are not haiku."

MERWIN: Well, they aren't haiku.

ELLIOTT: No, They aren't. But, on the other hand, they seem to be haiku-informed, so to speak, and doing a lot of the same things that haiku do.

MERWIN: I would like them to do some of the same things.

ELLIOTT: And I don't mean just that they are three lines long.

MERWIN: A lot of haiku, as you know, were never written as three lines; they were written as one line. I did want to try to do some of the same things that I think haiku do in Japanese, but of course I don't know what haiku do in Japanese because I don't read Japanese, and I'm less than satisfied with most translations of haiku. With many translations of mine, what started me translating was a sense that there was a poem behind the existing translation that wasn't making it into English, and I wanted to try to make a translation into English that did carry it over. I probably didn't succeed any better than any of the other translators, but I would have liked them to do some of the things that I imagine haiku would do in the original. I wasn't trying to follow a set of rules, but I was intrigued by the notion of the linked haiku that Basha and some of his disciples were writing, and that was what made me think of joining a series of them so that they played off against each other and made a larger whole. It made a kind of context.

ELLIOTT: Would you ever consider doing a renga? Have you ever toyed with the possibility?

MERWIN: I've considered it, but it never got very far. In our society, it seems like a game. There was a very interesting article on them as a kind of spiritual practice in the last issue of *Eastern Buddhist*. But I can remember being interested in very short verse forms because of the speed with which they seem to travel and the sort of lightning flash that they are. They're there in quite a number of traditions, some in Spanish— very short poems. I translated some of them back in the fifties.

ELLIOTT: I've noticed in some of the haiku journals that more and more people seem to be taking haiku as a jumping-off point and writing three-line, two-line, or one-line poems that probably would not be officially thought of as haiku at all by the conservative schools of haiku in Japan.

MERWIN: I love the thought of haiku as being a jumping-off point, considering Basho's frog.

ELLIOTT: What did you think of Robert Aitken's including the transliterations of Basho's haiku along with the translations and then trying to talk the reader through the various meanings of the words?

MERWIN: I think transliteration is a very good idea. I'm not talking about Aitken's now, but there are books where the transliteration is much more exciting than the translation.

ELLIOTT: Are the translations you're doing of Dōgen's poetry posing quite a challenge?

MERWIN: I'm working with Kazuaki Tanahashi, who knows very well what Dōgen is talking about, and the basic situation with many of his poems we've been translating is very simple. Students of Dōgen's will come to him with portraits of Dōgen and ask him to write a little poem on them; many of them are little poems about portraits of him. And it's a wonderful starting point for Dōgen to make up the poems.

ELLIOTT: Another book that certainly comes to mind in talking about short forms is *Asian Figures*. In the foreword to that book you talk in terms of the "urge to finality of utterance, . . . and to be irreducible and unchangeable" [vii], as if such poems are little units that perhaps have an integrity that longer poems begin to lose. But is there the problem, when writing haiku or your three-line poems, that you could fall into just making a little set piece, like one little jewel?

MERWIN: I think it is a problem. I think the urge that you are talking about could be an urge to find something that is as near absolute as you can get in language. I think that's okay, but you don't want to be stuck with that either. You don't want to paint yourself into a corner. Language is articulation of something, but we don't know what it's articulation of. Finally it's an attempt to say what we are, to say what our experience is to us, and we can't be absolute about that. So the urge to say something undeformable, unchangeable, irreversible is a very important urge, but it's only one, and the tension is set up by the fact that there is an opposite urge too, which is to be articulate, and to expatiate, to be discursive, to do all of those things. At regular intervals the writing of poetry in general does tend to become extremely prolix, the way traditions get very discursive, very diluted and diffuse, and the other pole is lost sight of. But you can get so succinct that there is nothing left.

ELLIOTT: Did you finally stop writing those three-line poems? You have written short poems at various times in your career, but certainly it seems as if all of a sudden there were a great many of them and then in *Opening the Hand* probably fewer short poems than in your other major collections of poetry. Have you written out that shortness?

MERWIN: Yes. I think the short ones really had all gone into those two collections in *Finding the Islands*.

ELLIOTT: Was there then a tension in your own writing between the more discursive, which comes out in *Opening the Hand*, and that temptation to be as succinct as possible?

MERWIN: Probably. There are poems that try to do both, like the questionnaire poem, about the pineapple. Every one of the questions has a completeness of its own.

ELLIOTT: In *A Zen Wave,* Robert Aitken says that "like . . . Basho, we must use words. How should we use them? By playing with them. . . . The purpose is to present something, not to mean something. Meaning something destroys it" [127]. Is that, you think, one of those difficult lessons that many Western poets cannot come to terms with?

MERWIN: You can push that too far and you end up with the post-phenomenologists saying that there is no subject and that there is no need for a subject, that the poetry need have no relationship to any subject. The poem is on its own, apart from anything. Something that seems to me fairly obvious is that both things are true: the poem does exist on its own, but that doesn't mean the poem has no relation to a subject. These two apparently contradictory things are actually happening at the same time. The poem is not the same thing as the subject. The poem would also not exist *without* the subject. The two have an essential relationship; and I really can't imagine being interested in a poem that doesn't have a subject, some kind of subject.

ELLIOTT: How about the Language poets?

MERWIN: Well, if you like games just for the sake of games . . . I find them boring after a while—after a fairly short while.

ELLIOTT: Because their subject is just themselves?

MERWIN: I really want a poem to make the world stop, for a matter of a few seconds.

ELLIOTT: Why is it, do you think, that such poets seem to be interested in going on beyond the traditional role for poetry, as if saying, "Well, that's been done. For poetry to go forward it has to be doing something completely different?"

MERWIN: True originality has to do not with trying to be new but trying to come from the place from which all renewal comes. The meaning or originality has to do with origin, the place where something comes from, not the fact that it is different from everything else. You can't be different from everything else. It's like saying life must do something quite new. It is doing something quite new all the time.

The Language poets clearly want something out of poetry that is different from what I want out of poetry. Why that should be so I can guess, but I certainly don't know. I haven't talked to them about it. I think it's very decadent. It's what you do when you haven't got anything to do.

ELLIOTT: So are we into another fin-de-siecle period, and that's the form of decadence that our poetry is taking?

21

MERWIN: Maybe. I wonder whether there's a certain numbness involved. At a time when there is tremendous urgency, to say there must be no urgency in poetry, of all arts! We don't know what speech is for. Every time we speak we are finding out a little bit more about what the words are for. Speech is for speaking, speech is for saying.

ELLIOTT: In your poetry you refer to names quite frequently, to things "with their names" and other things "without their names." In, *The Compass Flowe,* there are two or three images that are somewhat similar: "The beginning / comes from before / when the words for it were pictures of strangers / it comes on wings that never waited for their names" ["Kore"; 511], or "the rain whose ancestors / with no names / made the valley" ["June Rain"; 69]. What is it that naming does?

MERWIN: It sets up a concept between you and what you are looking at. The cat doesn't know it's a cat until you teach it that it is a cat.

ELLIOTT: And then by setting up that concept do we feel that we have possession over it?

MERWIN: I think so. We feel that we have some control over it. The names are important to us; we can't do without them. But on the other hand you can be trapped in the names and they can keep that barrier between you and things. I don't know his writing very well, but I believe that Heidegger talks about that.

ELLIOTT: Heidegger and Sartre both trace back to Husserl, but Sartre seems somehow to regret and yet accept as unavoidable the distance which naming and language create between us and the phenomenal world, whereas Heidegger and Buddhism go beyond that. Getting back to the Language poets, might they be working out of that frustration with the separation?

MERWIN: We can't live without concepts, but it's important to notice that they're concepts.

ELLIOTT: So then when you say things like "with no names," in a sense you are talking about a relationship between you and something else where you are able to perceive the suchness directly; there is no name interposed, no concept of your own which you think somehow draws it into you.

MERWIN: Well, there is an evocation of the thing that is there before there's a name, before there's a concept of it. The rain falls whether we know it's rain falling or not.
ELLIOTT: Is it something like the practice of sitting in meditation that gives us what we need to separate things from their names?

MERWIN: Then you might notice whether what you are seeing is the rain falling or your idea of the rain falling.

ELLIOTT: It's in images and lines such as the ones referring to names that the parallel between your poetry and Buddhism is evident, but it is put there in terms that do not force the reader to think, "That's Buddhist."

MERWIN: I would not want it to be put there in those terms. In fact even in translating Dōgen we are trying to find our way around using words like "dharma."

ELLIOTT: In other words, you would like these translations to exist without a need for a glossary.

MERWIN: Yes, without the need for a special vocabulary, which means a prejudiced set of assumptions about it, like "Dharma is a good thing."

ELLIOTT: Twentieth-century poets who come to mind in terms of Eastern influence are first of all Eliot and Pound, both in rather idiosyncratic ways. Are there any other poets in the twentieth century American tradition who you think have been influenced in a positive way by Eastern thought or Buddhism?

MERWIN: I suspect that Stevens was. I don't know that, but poems like "The Snow Man" and "A Rabbit As King of the Ghosts" and "The River of Rivers in Connecticut," a quite late one and a poem that I love, seem to me to be very marked by it. I don't know whether this was deliberate. I don't believe that such insight is the monopoly of any "ism." I think that it's a basic way of seeing the world which Buddhism happened to articulate in a particularly clear way. But it's human. For that matter, it may not even be just human; it may be mammalian. It may be vertebrate.

ELLIOTT: But it does seem as if Western civilization did a better job of repressing it for a long period of time than Eastern civilization.

MERWIN: We set up dualism which obscures it. I understand that Stevens had a Buddha in his study. I don't know what that means. He may have had it there for decorative purposes.

ELLIOTT: I'm glad you said what you did about "The Snow Man" because I think that gets back to what we were talking about a while ago, about how the concept of emptiness has traditionally been seen in the West as something to fear. I've seen many interpretations of "The Snow Man" that tried to turn it into a very negative poem. It does seem more like a Buddhist emptiness.

MERWIN: I think it's an exhilarating poem. What happens if one is going to see that poem as a negative poem, as a depressing and finally a despairing poem, is that you start thinking too fast about those last lines before you've really taken them in. You start setting up a defense about them and analyzing them before you've really listened to them.

ELLIOTT: Is there something categorically different about Dōgen's poems when compared to a poem like "The Snow Man"? In other words, is there a way in which those poems are probably going to be more remote to the Western mind?

MERWIN: I don't know. I think that late poem of Dōgen's about snow, for example, is no more remote than Stevens's "Snow Man" and is really not very different in its purport.

ELLIOTT: I'd like to see that one.

MERWIN: It was written a year before he died, when he was in his fifties. It goes,

> All my life tangled
> in false and real
> right and wrong
> playing with the moon
> laughing at wind
> listening to birds
> year after year wasted seeing

24

          a mountain covered
              with snow
          only this winter
       I know that the snow
          is the mountain

ELLIOTT: I'd like to return to your recent poetry. Before the publication of *Opening the Hand* you said that you were thinking of removing from the poem "Coming Back in the Spring" a specific reference to IRA hunger strikers [Folsom and Nelson 48]. Now, I don't know what you might have taken out, but you mention an IRA hunger striker in that poem.

MERWIN: They are all there.

ELLIOTT: So you didn't take anything out? Are you happy with that decision now?

MERWIN: I am *now*. But it's not a matter of principle. Some things just don't seem to work. Sometimes it takes a long time before you can tell with any kind of certainty yourself whether they really work or not. My wish to have those things in the poem may not have had much to do with the poem. It may have been from outside the poem. I may have been self-indulgent. That was what my misgiving was concerned with. And then I became finally satisfied that it did belong in the poem, that it did seem to work.

ELLIOTT: But does your leaving those specific references in the poem come from a different response to the present political turmoil than the one you had in the sixties? Is your feeling one of, "OK, here we go again, and maybe this time I should leave in some of the specifics instead of withholding them or not allowing them to enter in"?

MERWIN: Well, I would like to be able to write them in such a way that I can feel they belong there. I don't think that just because I've got the particulars I can decide to put them into the poem and it will make the poem good. There is an awful lot of bad poetry written that way. And it doesn't matter how much one agrees with the intent. The poem can still be bad.

ELLIOTT: I wonder if we are not far from a time when, as in the sixties, there are going to be more poets writing topical poems and rallying around some current political causes.

MERWIN: I just hope that they and we can make them poems, because the urge to write propaganda is one that I not only understand but that I sympathize with. But I think it is an urge that doesn't make poems very often.

ELLIOTT: But as propaganda, you are willing to let it have its short life?

MERWIN: Oh sure. It's better than not saying anything. And the occasional political poem that works is sometimes a very great poem, and sometimes a very funny poem. You know that poem, by Ernesto Cardenál, about all the dreadful things that are going on in Nicaragua. All the babies are crying and the people are fighting with each other. And the last line is "Somoza is driving through town."

ELLIOTT: There seems to be a listlessness in much contemporary poetry.

MERWIN: About political issues?

ELLIOTT: Yes.

MERWIN: A listlessness about what's really going on. There is a terrible temptation, a terrible danger of preaching. But there is an awful lot of frivolity too and that sort of fluff—part of that same decadence we were talking about.

ELLIOTT: Would you like to talk about your current writing on Hawaii?

MERWIN: We were talking earlier about intent. You never know what you've written, and you forget what you intended. You know at a given time what you want to write, but it's never what you end up writing. I have been thinking about this in the last year, partly because of the great satisfaction and excitement of working on what I've been doing, which seems to me to gather together things that I've been wanting to do since before I could read and write, for reasons I don't altogether understand in a rational way, having a certain amount to do with the culture of Hawaiian people, and with a non-European, non-literate life, all of it happening at a time indeed when the culture seems to be doomed and disappearing.

ELLIOTT: The Hawaiian culture?

MERWIN: Well, what culture isn't? But the Hawaiian culture is under terrible menace. There are no Hawaiians who don't speak English and many Hawaiians who don't speak Hawaiian. Draw your own conclusions. The land has been taken away and the culture has been downgraded and kept in pockets on the island. But being able to have any closeness and any relation to it—to me it's a great fulfillment. And to realize that that relation has come into direct conflict with the things that I have long been in conflict with myself . . . I mean the destruction of the natural world and the destruction of other cultures, the kind of military and technological arrogance of our culture and our time. And in fact it's happening all over the Pacific. The Pacific to me historically is now the focus of history. For years for me it was New York; but now it really seems to be somewhere in the Pacific, probably on the uninhabited island of Kahoolawe, which the Navy is bombing.

ELLIOTT: Just routinely, as practice?

MERWIN: Routinely, every year. It is the sacred island of the Hawaiians and is covered with archeological sites.

ELLIOTT: How long has this been going on?

MERWIN: Since 1939. They were about to stop it when the Hawaiian people asked to have the island back. But they stepped it up. That's the basis for the story. But in order to write it you have to figure out what the involvement of the Hawaiian people on that island has been right through to the present and then what the involvement of the Navy has been. It's history in a sense, the kind of writing I suppose would go in the same genre with something like the books of Peter Matthiessen. I'm just trying to tell the story fairly straight.

ELLIOTT: And you are tape-recording conversations with people to find out their feelings about this?

MERWIN: Their lives as they've had to do with this island.

ELLIOTT: So you see it as a book-length manuscript?

MERWIN: I didn't start it that way. I started it as a neat little essay. And there are a lot of other aspects of the situation that I think of as nice essays of about forty pages, but who knows? I mean there is so much of that story that has never been told. When the old people start talking on this, it streams out, they talk so well.

ELLIOTT: Do you see Hawaii as being permanent in your life? You've lived in France, you've lived in Mexico, and New York has always been a sort of coming back place.

MERWIN: I feel very much at home there. I love it. One of the other things I've become involved in is trying to grow and save endangered species of trees and plants. That has a history too of its own. Hawaii is unique. The flora and fauna that were there when Captain Cook got there were almost entirely exclusive to Hawaii. They had almost all evolved there. There's no other place on earth where this is true. There is still no place on earth which is as priceless a laboratory for studying evolution as the Hawaiian islands, and they have been raped and torn apart by large scale exploitative agriculture.

ELLIOTT: Given the current political and ecological crises, do you feel the impulse to write more occasional pieces of a political nature, such as those you wrote for *The Nation* in the sixties?

MERWIN: This enormous thing that I seem to be in the middle of is that. I mean it is political because you can't write about this subject unpolitically, apolitically. I've come to believe that there is scarcely any such thing as the Russian military and the American military. I believe that deeper than that there is the world military, and they are mutually sustaining.

ELLIOTT: Did the people you interviewed in Hawaii seem to have concerns that went beyond simply the concern for that particular sacred island?

MERWIN: We were on the island in May. The Navy allows them to go over on a part of the island once a month. The organization is called the Protect Kahoolawe Ohana, which now is the focus organization for the Hawaiian consciousness; and we went over at the end of May with a bunch of people from all around the Pacific, people from Belau, New Caledonia, the Marshall Islands, the Philippines, New Zealand, Maui.

This is something which is happening now very fast around the Pacific. There have already been two pan-Pacific conferences organized by the Independent Nuclear-free Pacific, mainly indigenous people saying, "We are tired of being rubbed out and we insist on our own identity, our own culture, and the Pacific nature of our culture, and we don't want to be part of the Russian bloc, the Chinese bloc, or any other bloc; we're Pacific, and we don't want the nuclear threat here in any form: we don't want nuclear missiles, we don't want nuclear dumping, we don't want nuclear tests, we don't want nuclear stockpiling." How far it will go, who knows? But it's growing and the State Department doesn't like it very much. As one of the guys in the diplomatic corps said, "They don't understand that it is unacceptable to our strategy." A nuclear-free Pacific, that is. I had the feeling very strongly on Kahoolawe in May that this was the center, where it was all happening, on this empty island in the Pacific.

ELLIOTT: Much of what you've said brings to mind the concluding lines to "The River of Bees": "we were not born to survive / Only to live" [*Lice* 33].

MERWIN: That again has been described as an incredibly bleak and negative point of view. I don't think of it that way.

ELLIOTT: Is losing attachment to survival something that might be needed in order to survive?

MERWIN: I think it is important to pay attention to living rather than to surviving, if we can. I mean, surviving doesn't mean very much if your life doesn't mean very much, does it?

Notes

Aitken, Robert. *A Zen Wave*. Foreword W.S. Merwin. New York: Weatherhill, 1978.

Auden, W.H. Foreword. *A Mask for Janus*. W.S. Merwin. New Haven: Yale, 1952.

Dōgen. "Snow." Trans. Kazuaki Tanahashi and David Schneider. Adapted W.S. Merwin.

Folsom, Ed and Cary Nelson. "'Fact Has Two Faces': An Interview with W.S. Merwin." *Iowa Review* 13.1 (1982): 30-66.

Merwin, W.S. *Asian Figures*. New York: Atheneum, 1973.

_____. *The Carrier of Ladders*. New York: Atheneum, 1970.

_____. *The Compass Flower*. New York: Atheneum, 1977.

_____. *The Lice*. New York: Atheneum, 1967.

II. At Home in the Dark

A Conversation with William Stafford

La Plume, Pennsylvania
March 1988

William Stafford (1914-1993) published over 50 books of poetry, large and small, including *Traveling Through the Dark* , which won the National Book Award. He was appointed Consultant in Poetry to the Library of Congress (later known as Poet Laureate) in 1970.

ELLIOTT: As I was looking through your books in preparation for this interview, I realized that there are certain words I associate with much of your poetry, and so I want to throw some of these words out to you one at a time to see how you react. I'd like to know your feelings about them with regard to anything that comes to your mind, not necessarily just in relation to your poetry. I make it sound like this is going to be a Freudian free association test.

STAFFORD: It will be. I'm not afraid.

ELLIOTT: The first word is "dream."

STAFFORD: As soon as you say that, I realize that word gets into my poems sometimes. I'm not aware of its being remarkably prevalent in my poems, but I immediately thought of the poem that says, "This dream the world is having about itself," or something like that ("Vocation," *Stories* 107). It's kind of a treacherous word for me as a writer because it's like one of those exits-from-trouble words you can use. You know: "I dreamed it . . . " Just a way of smuggling in something that you want to put in and it signifies a state of consciousness or state of being that is exempted from some of the rules or elements in actuality. Mostly I want to be a person who inhabits actuality, so "dream" is a troublesome word to me, even if I use it.

ELLIOTT: At times the word can be too fuzzy, so to speak?

STAFFORD: Yes, it can be too fuzzy, but in this poem, "Early Morning," for example, there is no other word that will do: "Inside this dream to come awake . . . . " When I say this I am affirming my conviction or my realization that we are fooling ourselves when we think we have got control of our lives and of the things that surface in our minds. ·
So:

> Inside this dream to come awake,
> be held above the ground, have air
> catch me, then fall onward and know
> it is a dream, then wake and be falling—

I love this dream, God, where
in a dream You have me dream
You, and come quiet into this place
and be Your waking

(*Smoke's Way* 67)

To me it's just satisfyingly complex, convoluted into a "what's it all about?" kind of feeling.

ELLIOTT: Let's move on. I'm not necessarily coming up with words that appear in many, many poems, but just ones that caught my attention.

STAFFORD: Well, that would be interesting. I'll psychoanalyze you. Which words occurred to you? [Laughing.]

ELLIOTT: OK, here's the next one: "wind." You have a lot of wind in your poems.

STAFFORD: I do have a *lot* of wind in my poems, and I don't feel nervous about that. If I were trying to write poems that austerely stayed clear of each other it might worry me, but I'm not. In my writing I'm willing to be obsessed, if obsessed I am. That's what my writing's about. I'll drop a word when it no longer occurs to me, but not before, and "wind" for me is a handy word. For one thing I grew up in Kansas, and I remember being back there a couple of years ago. I walked out in the morning. It wasn't wind exactly; it's just that all the air in the world was going somewhere else. And so it's not surprising that someone in Kansas would have wind and sky and land. That's what's there. And someone who didn't have much wind in their concepts or talk or world would think this is artificial business. I'm just facing reality.

ELLIOTT: You were talking about Yeats earlier today, and I would imagine that you might be resistant to someone who, when dealing with your poetry, tried to make a neat equation between this word and some pre-existing concept, the way that "gyre" in Yeats can trigger a set response. But I'm wondering how you react to my feeling that when wind gets mentioned in several poems, it seems to be associated with changes.

STAFFORD: It's something I hadn't myself made a linkage with, but it sounds all right to me. I mean, my quick assessment says, "Well, I believe you have something there." I would be resistant about equating these words to certain concepts or even recurrent things in my life, because for me, when I'm writing, a word is something that happens to come along and be handy in the context where it occurs to me; and that context might be enough different so my use of the word would make it a different thing, because of the context. Even when I seem to be doing something that is just a broken record, the word feels different to me because it comes in at a different pace or a different place in life and the progress of my considerings. So I have this weird idea that some of those words that a person would identify in my poems (this is a humiliating thing to confess) are just little blips that I put in, because I have used them often enough before—they're lying around—and I don't know what to put in there so I use one. It's like a blank thing in some of these games, you know, counters that you can move. This can stand for anything. I need one syllable here, so "wind" comes in. And someone says, "There it is again; see that's the same idea." Well, it's just that I was more desperate this time, maybe.

ELLIOTT: How about "darkness"?

STAFFORD: "Darkness" I was even aware of in the reading today because someone recently told me that "dark" and "darkness" show up in my poems, and I believe they were saying (contrary to what I just said about how "wind" was only a counter to get one syllable in there) that the word carries a large part of my way of adjusting to the world. It is a label for an element that is prevalent in my writing. I think that's true. For me there is a characteristic that I feel in my writing, and in my life and that is an abiding reconciliation with the idea that I am so limited, that I am operating in a world that I can't control. There are a lot of things out there I don't know anything about. And there's another thing I will say about this. There is a little aggression in this too, and that is I don't think other people know about a lot of those things either. So when people say something or act in a way that suggests to me that they have forgotten that limit, I lose faith in them and what they are saying.

ELLIOTT: There are two poems of yours that almost seem companion poems in terms of dealing with darkness: first, one that you may get tired of people talking about all the time—"Traveling Through the Dark," perhaps your best-known poem. And one that I associate with it, "A Ritual to Read to Each Other": "The darkness around us is deep" (*Stories* 52).

STAFFORD: That is such a flat statement at the end that I know I should be nervous about it. I think I have been taught that I should be nervous about it. But I do not naturally feel nervous about it; it is just a pretty forthright way of saying what I guess I was fumbling to say earlier—"the darkness around us is deep"—and some people don't know that, but I'm reconciled to it. And there is one other little thing: I'm sort of glad. I mean, I feel at home in the dark where I live.

ELLIOTT: Is it sometimes dark where the wolves might be that you're piling up the stones to . . .

STAFFORD: [Laughing.] I'm afraid that was fairly mechanical, a thing that got into my poem ["Things That Come"], because even the wolves are friendly, actually. There are quite a number of wolves in my poems. Sometimes I'm using the wolf in the conventional way, you know, the slaughterer of the lambs; but sometimes I'm using it as the friendly beast who helps keep you warm in the dark when there is a storm. Same word, but . . .

ELLIOTT: Here's another one: "glimpse."

STAFFORD: Yes. There is a pattern in these words, I suddenly realize. A wind is moving and you can't count on any certain thing it is going to do, just that it's going to keep on being there. Darkness is a limit on our realizations, and a glimpse is about as far as I can go in looking. I mean a glimpse is a limited look and our insights are limited; they are glimpses. So it's almost as if there is a little configuration of words that bear on each other. It's no wonder they show up, since they signify as a group, in their relation to each other, some kind of perception, or perhaps delusion (but my own) about the world and our situation in it—that it's a glimpsy place, it's a windy place, it's surrounded by darkness, but even the darkness is friendly. I said earlier it's not that I'm worried about the dark; I like it.

ELLIOTT: Another word that came to mind is "friend," which you were saying something about in the questions after the reading. You told the story about friends you don't really like. But friends show up in more positive and conventional ways in many of your poems.

36

STAFFORD: Yes, this seems paradoxical, but I feel easy about the idea that some of my friends I don't like very well [Laughing] because a friend is more important than assessment. There is a location, there is a home place for your feelings with a friend, and you don't necessarily assess friends as admirable or that you especially *like* them; but they are a part of the world you count on. They're there; you have located them. You have repeated glimpses of them and you can go part way into the dark with them.

Let me say one other thing about "friend." It's complicated, I think, for me to assess what the word "friend" means, because in my life there have been crucial episodes in which capital "F" Friend (Quaker) positions—like "Speak truth to power," and the importance of social and personal company in a world surrounded by darkness—have been important to me. There have been capital "F" Friends. Also, in-group friends in a world where the out-group is a big strong group and the in-group is a minority in need of friends.

ELLIOTT: Let me pursue the capital "F" Friend a little bit more. When William Heyen interviewed you he referred to you as a Quaker and that was the only time I have ever heard that word applied to you. Was he just assuming that you were a Quaker because of your pacifism, or have you actually had some formal relationship with them?

STAFFORD: I forgot Heyen said that. But if that would go past in a conversation and someone would just say about me, "He's a Quaker," that's as good a way as any to identify me, because language is sort of loose and shifting. Someone outside the Peace Movement, for instance, might think maybe everyone in the Peace Movement is a Quaker; and if that's the way they use the word, why should I stop and say, "Wait, let's stop and talk about Fox and the history of Quakerism"? So it's kind of a loose label, one that's as good as any for people who don't know distinctions among Friends and Mennonites, Brethren, and in my four years when I was a conscientious objector during World War II, I was in Church of Brethren camps and ended up working at the headquarters for the Church of the Brethren. But for most people "Quaker" covers all that. So if we say, "Is it true I'm a Quaker?" no, I'm not a Quaker. The social action part of Quakerism, that's what I was doing before there were any Quakers where I lived. When I got where they were, we were doing the same thing, and when Dorothy and I have lived where there is a Quaker meeting, we have often gone.

37

ELLIOTT: Another word on my list, which is apropos now, is "quiet."

STAFFORD: I even have a collection called *The Quiet of Land.* One place on this circuit, I read a poem of mine called "On a Church Lawn." It's dandelion seeds that speak. They mention to each other "their dandelion faith: 'God is not big, he is right'" (*Stories* 14). I have this feeling of being at the right place at the right time with the right attitude when I am something the opposite of saying or claiming more or asserting more, but instead being quiet. Maybe this still small voice is here somewhere, something like that. I don't know; "quiet" is one of my words.

ELLIOTT: Is there any connection between your attitude toward quiet and silence and your own method of writing? I know you talk about getting up early in the morning to be alone in a quiet situation, but is there a form of inner quietness which provides a more fertile ground, to mix metaphors, for your poems to come out of?

STAFFORD: I think so; I mean I feel congenial to what you just said, partly because for me the experience of finding the way in writing is one of sensitivity, listening, glimpsing, going forward by means of little signals, and those little signals are available in conditions of quiet, lack of turbulence, and conditions that are non-confrontational. Thinking, forensic thinking, is a nonsense term to me. I think that one finds one's way with a sensibility that requires an attitude other than loudness or aggression. I'm sort of surprised to be talking about this because we're talking about writing, but now we are talking about an attitude, and I guess it shows up recurrently in the writing. Even the images would be clues to this attitude. When I write I don't feel I'm trying to put forward an attitude or a position, but I realize it's there.

ELLIOTT: With regard to silence and quiet: in a certain way Hindu meditation, with the concept of a mantra, is trying to fill your mind up with sound; but certain Buddhist meditations are in a sense trying to empty it out and deal with more quietness. The quietness of Zen meditation, the quietness of the Quaker meeting—those seem to me to be very compatible. Is there a way in which poetry for you could be considered a type of meditation?

STAFFORD: Yes, I think so. Partly I'm lagging behind you because I'm fascinated by that idea of maybe two different kinds of people: those who want to fill up their mind in order to have whatever it is you get, and those who want to have the quiet there. I would side with the second group. Yes, poetry for me is much like meditation in the sense that writing is cultivating a state of receptivity and following what suggests itself out of that quiet state. I hadn't thought of putting it this strongly, but it's meditation that allows itself to be manifest in written language. Rather than just the unembodied meditation going on, the impulse is to maximize the effect of meditation by allowing it to become manifest in something that lasts on the page.

ELLIOTT: In your essays about writing, the faith that somehow there is that within everyone which can manifest itself in writing and in an authentic way seems to be very comfortable for you. A lot of people would say a leap of faith is needed for that.

STAFFORD: It *is* comfortable for me, I think, for a number of reasons. For instance Kierkegaard has this: everybody's equal, not in the Jeffersonian sense, but *equal*, in the face of the magnitude of what we don't know. Human presumption about the more or less is quaint; you know, it's provincial, it's a provinciality to make much of that. I wrote an article called "A Priest of the Imagination." I guess it's in *You Must Revise Your Life*. But I wrote it to give at a gathering of English teachers, and in there there is this faith, this idea: I'm a priest of the imagination and when I go to class my job is conducting the inner light of those people to wherever it's going. I remember the argument it started among the English teachers.

ELLIOTT: To get back to my list of words, another one that seems to show up now and again in different forms is "awake" or "waking."

STAFFORD: Yes. You certainly have made me conscious of a configuration of words that I really hadn't thought of like this. But waking, or the state of being awake, is for me that condition in the life of a limited creature that is possible with a glimpse. Coming awake is coming out of ignorance and darkness into some kind of awareness. But even the condition of being awake is not really being awake to what's there; there's no way to penetrate or encompass fully the mysteries that are around us.

ELLIOTT: In "Early Morning" you say, "Let me be Your waking," and the "Y" is the capital "Y," God (*Smoke's Way* 67). That sounds like a heavy responsibility.

STAFFORD: [Laughing] Yes, there is a lot of swagger in there, isn't there? To me it's a strange mixture, because the capital "Y" signifies "Your Eminence," but meanwhile I'm being the conduit somehow. I didn't know how to avoid the obligation in my poems, so at least temporarily I just shouldered it.

ELLIOTT: Here's another word, and I guess I'm moving to ones that are much more abstract: "time."

STAFFORD: Yes. A book I'm carrying along on this circuit is *Confessions of Saint Augustine*, and he has in there a sophisticated, subtle analysis of time. It's just one of the mysteries. By the way, I was in a conversation with a priest the other night who asked me what I was carrying. I said, "I'm carrying the *Confessions of Saint Augustine*." I felt good about saying that to him. But then he said, "What else?" and I said "Nietzsche's *Beyond Good and Evil*." [Laughing.] Both of them fascinating, and Nietzsche actually occured to me earlier on some issue. One of the things he says is, "Every word is a prejudice."

ELLIOTT: You play around with time a lot in your poetry.

STAFFORD: That's true. Time shows up in things like "The Rescued Year," one of my poems where the train comes in and backs out, and so time comes in and then it goes backwards. But, for me, the fascinating part of writing is the juggling of these puzzles, being enticed forward to consider insoluble problems, to make poems out of them and not to presume to be able to solve them. I'm willingly dazzled by perennial puzzles. Sometimes in my poems I may pretend to have it, solve it. Believe me, I do not have those presumptions; it's just for the duration of the poem. It's for the poem's sake.

ELLIOTT: Over the last twenty years or so there have been a lot of poems that use the word "you": "You do this, you do that." With many poets I get the idea that really it's just a thinly disguised "I." I don't get that feeling out of most of your poems. One of the things the voice of your poetry seems to do is that when you say "you"—"you might do this," "someday this might happen to you," and so on—it makes me feel as if somehow you've got your finger on archetypal situations, certain patterns of being in the world which you have been able to recognize; and you are throwing these things out to people, saying, "Be on the lookout; this could happen to you too." And I often feel that this "you" really is me, or could be. Another way of saying this is that in the voice of your poetry you make a real connection with the reader.

STAFFORD: I like what you said. I would like to claim it, but I wouldn't like to overclaim it. I mean I'm willing to be vulnerable on this. In fact, the idea of avoiding "I" has occurred to me a number of times when I'm writing, but there are various ways to do that. Even a poem I read today says, "Tell me, you years I had for my life, / tell me . . . ("Remembering Brother Bob," *Glass Face* 91). Well, that was to me liberating phrasing, because it enabled me to have something else ask these things. So I'm aware of that.

On the other hand, I believe that the going over into the other person, the "you"—really doing it, or more than some people might— could have happened to me, maybe, because of actual circumstances in my life. For instance, several places in my poems I say something about how my mother couldn't hear very well, and she couldn't. It became a part of my second nature to be aware of a person in a group who was excluded from the group by anything, including not hearing what's going on. I mean, that's almost like a metaphor. Many people can't hear; even if their ears are all right, they don't know what's going on. So if you're a teacher, you have a responsibility for these people in outer darkness to bring them in. I would rephrase things in her presence so she would hear them instead of thinking maybe she heard them. And there's this inhabiting somebody else's presence in a scene, partly with my own consciousness, in order to include that person. As teachers we do this, as someone who hears when somebody else doesn't hear, as someone maybe who understands when someone else doesn't understand.

ELLIOTT: Getting back to the word "glimpse" . . . It seems as if in your poetry you are often passing on to the reader what may be the significant glimpses in your own life. I know you resist thinking that way because you talk about simply playing out possibilities in your writing, but some of those possibilities seem to play out in ways that other people can read and say, "That sounds wise," as opposed to, "He's just playing around with ideas."

STAFFORD: That is right. Let me stop and sort of stir this around a little bit. First, I just recognized what I had already referred to even in this conversation and which is recurrent when I think about writing—my feeling of being reckless, just taking whatever the language suggests to me, not being responsible. It is true though (I don't know how to reconcile this) that I feel great satisfaction and then eagerness to have my poems be not just dances of language but also, or maybe even more so (or maybe there is a convergence here) dances that also get you there. And I'd like to get there. And if someone says, and they have, and cruelly sometimes, "Stafford, stay out of my life; quit telling me how to live. The little ways that encourage good fortune, *you* figure that out. I'll figure out my own ways," I don't feel hurt about that. They don't really mean it. They need help. [Laughing.] There are doctrinaire people who say that it doesn't belong in poetry and they'd kick out a lot of the Bible and so on. I'll take my stand, with the good book.

ELLIOTT: On the one hand, you write certain poems that maybe can give us glimpses of, let's say, wisdom, and on the other hand you've got this "But I'm just playing with imagination" point of view. So it seems your poetry does both things, and sometimes those approaches are congruent and sometimes they aren't, and you don't want to cut yourself off from either one.

STAFFORD: Yes. There is another little quirk that I think of and that is, though I would be quite willing for my poems to be gems of truth and guides for people [chuckling], as for myself I would feel quite wary of treating anybody else's poems as guides. I think of a formulation for this: "Prove all things; hold fast that which is good." And when I read somebody else, I'm not holding fast to everything they say; I'm proving all things. But when I find myself falling in step with them I'm delighted, and if someone else falls in step with me, we both have to have "maybe" in our life still, but there is a feeling of company for a little while.

ELLIOTT: Another word that doesn't show up as much in your poetry (although it is the first word of your first collection) but which seems present in the content of your work, is "West." Your new book is entitled *An Oregon Message*. You have said that you don't feel that you're really a poet of place. You like when people converge with the landscape, but that could be anywhere and there is nothing special about Oregon (Stafford, *You Must* 61). It is true that an awful lot of your poetry doesn't really connect with a particular place. In many of the poems the natural world occurs only in generalized terms. But is there a sense of space in your work, perhaps, which a Western poet, from Kansas or Oregon, might understandably have? Your poems aren't crowded. They certainly aren't urban, and it seems as if in many Eastern poets there is a sense of crowdedness, whereas in many Western poets there is a greater sense of space. Does that make any sense for either your own poetry or anybody else's you know?

STAFFORD: Yes. I feel two topics crowding in on me here. One is that the existence of the feeling many people have about this—the common acceptance of the West as being open and new and out with the hand clasp a little stronger, and so on—is so strong that it's available, when you write. It is like saying, "OK, you say I'm a Quaker, I'm a Quaker." You know, I just enter your world. And if you say I'm from the West, I'm from the West. The idea of the West is so handy that when you're casting about while you are writing, it would just limit you not to use it. I don't like to promote those ideas; I don't even know whether I believe them. But the beliefs of people are partly what you use when you write your poems, and you don't stop to revise their lives so that they can read a poem that drapes over actuality and have the experience they need to have. You just take their wrong impressions and let them use them: you pat them on the head and let them go ahead and plunge. So that's part of it.

The other topic is that whether or not inhabiting this metaphor or image of the West makes a difference in my writing, it makes a difference to me as a *person*. It's a part of what goes to make up those beliefs we were talking about. There is kind of a frontier irony. It's in Mark Twain, very much so. I don't want to be mean like Mark Twain, but there is a part of me that does laugh. Like when he says, "This is the great Christopher Columbus," and someone, the innocent, says, "Is he dead?" So I willingly inhabit that country undercutting of superiority from the more cultivated parts of any society, because this realization is congruent with my hunch about the condition of all of us. We are *all* limited, and the existence of a hierarchy, where a person is more likely to presume a knowledge or a full understanding, is like a target for someone out in the West. There's a kind of populist feeling about ideas even, rebellion against the presumption of knowledge or security. So I'm always plunging off into the wilderness happily, because that's what it really is anyway, wherever you are.

ELLIOTT: Here's another word, another abstraction: "acceptance."

43

STAFFORD: I think that shows up (I guess it does) in my vocabulary because it goes so congruently with this attitude I have toward the stance to take when doing art. It is the opposite of being austere, the opposite of holding off from intrusion into your process anything that might seem at the moment not worthy of what you are trying to do. So you accept what comes to you, you accept where you live, you accept the little hunches you have when you're writing because they may not have the validation of someone having them before or paying attention to them before, but they are the little waifs of emerging possibility that you pay attention to as one who works at the edge (in the West?) of what has already happened. You are in that area where it is now happening and you've got to use adobe if that's what's there. You have to use the teepee. You accept ramshackle ideas if they happen to come along. Now I'm getting too figurative. [Laughing.]

ELLIOTT: Many of your poems seem to be about missed opportunities.

STAFFORD: Yes, when you say it I realize I think that's right. There's something about the examined life (I'm improvising as I go) that would make it recurrently possible that you would have better hindsight than you have foresight. So you would think about these missed opportunities. I think that is also true in my life that I have the endemic feeling of not doing right. I mean I don't want to be this kind of person, I don't feel haunted, but I do certainly live with possible regrets, if I think about things. Even the poem "Ask Me"—"Some time . . . ask me / mistakes I have made . . . whether / what I have done is my life" (*Stories* 19). Well, what I have done isn't my life; it was trying to go somewhere else, and these mistakes I made made it happen. And in myself I'm aware of this. No, my life is really, I suppose, like other lives, no more confident, no more presuming of having chosen right, than even the most dismal poet who doesn't write things like, "Why I Am Happy." Some of those are like whistling in the dark—not "Traveling Through the Dark," but whistling in the dark.

And there is another thing I was thinking of (I just wanted to put it in—suddenly I feel sort of conscience-stricken). At the end of a circuit like this you travel and you meet people who have read the poems and you are sort of in a cocoon of accomplishment as you go. And then you come to the end of a circuit and you feel this great need for confession. You know, quite a bit of my writing has been published, but I think there are people who are assessing that writing now, who see it as a certain kind

44

of thing that was done, but it doesn't amount to all that much. I couldn't agree with them more. I believe that is right. I have no impulse to make the claims that implicitly I was accepting as I went around the circuit.

ELLIOTT: You were writing poems, not a canon.

STAFFORD: Yes, that's right. These were just things that came along. Whatever anyone says about them, I have no quarrel, not a bit. [Laughing.]

ELLIOTT: One last question. An idea associated with deconstructionist criticism, which is apparently bothering some creative writers who work in institutions where there are two factions—the creative writing faculty and the scholars—is that authors are in a sense not important. The language is writing the poem; not the author. There are certain ways in which that point of view is similar to some of the things you say about your writing process. Does that viewpoint seem to you to be compatible with yours? And if so, are there any other aspects of deconstruction that you are uncomfortable with?

STAFFORD: I do object to learning Esperanto in order to read those people. I have a feeling that we could approach each other much more helpfully if we would accept the language as it is and talk to each other about it. We should be much more ready to use ordinary language where we can and not force each other to go into the creation of lingo, even though I can see that if you're in something, there may be a language that is more apt for it and maybe you ought to learn it. But I haven't gotten any vibes from there that were very disturbing to me.

I often feel when I'm writing that I'm just present as the language crystallizes into a new poem, and if that is harmonious with deconstruction I'm ready for that. I had that feeling a long time ago. In a way I could have it in the envious way. You know, "Well, Keats was just lucky; he happened to be there ready when the language was just about to become 'Ode on a Grecian Urn.'" I try to get myself related to language in such a way as to encourage it to become what it's ready to become, and I feel compatible with that in many ways. For instance, I don't have this feeling of controlling the language but of just riding it wherever it's going. It's a social thing. Nobody invented it. Nobody that I'm aware of has real ability to guide it. We're going along with it. I feel that I'm sniffing my way forward into the development of the language.

45

Notes

Stafford, William. *A Glass Face in the Rain*. New York: Harper and Row, 1982.

_____. *Smoke's Way*. Port Townsend, WA: Greywolf Press, 1983.

_____. *Stories That Could Be True: New and Collected Poems*. New York: Harper and Row, 1977.

_____. *You Must Revise Your Life*. Poets on Poetry Series. Ann Arbor: University of Michigan Press, 1986.

When the William Stafford interview was published, it was edited for space. Those edited-out sections of the interview appeared in two different journals. We are including them here so you can read the entire interview as originally recorded.

The following excerpt is from "A Priest of the Imagination," published in Friends Journal, *November 1991.*

ELLIOTT: You are unusual among poets (among today's poets, at least) in that you held quite a variety of jobs before settling in academia. The list in *Contemporary Authors* ranges from soil conservation, farming, and the oil industry to the Brethren Service and the Church World Service. Could you expand a bit on that list?

STAFFORD: My work background has sometimes caused surprise among academics and writers. Once someone even asked me, "Why did you work in the sugar beet fields and in construction and so on?" I must have looked startled, for I thought people always worked at what was at hand; in our area (and it was dur ing the 1930s, come to think of it, when the depression was rampant) all of us sought out what jobs we could. I guess you could say we wanted to eat.

But I also liked the variety—Forest Service, oil refinery . . . What wonderful characters I met! And how good our lunch tasted, eaten in the shade of the car or huddled by big boilers or lounged along trails in the forest.

Then, as a result of serving as a conscientious objector during World War II, I naturally turned to relief work after the war, working alongside comrades from the camps, packing supplies in and around San Francisco for shipping abroad.

ELLIOTT: What were you doing immediately before the war?

STAFFORD: When I was drafted (in 1942, just a week or so after Pearl Harbor) I was well into my program toward a master's degree in English at the University of Kansas, and after my four years of captivity in the camps I went back and picked up the degree, with the help of my manuscript written during the time in camp. That manuscript became my first book, *Down in My Heart*, published by the Church of the Brethren, for whom I had served. The book was an account of those four years in camp.

ELLIOTT: You have said that on your way to the camp you had a copy of John Woolman's *Journal* with you.

STAFFORD: Right, my teacher gave me that as I was leaving. I don't think she talked directly to me about my being a conscientious objector. This was the time when people were scattering for military camps in all directions from the University of Kansas. But I thought about it later. I think she didn't say anything to me because there was no need to say anything. She was a Quaker and gave me *The Journal of John Woolman*, and when I read it, I saw.

ELLIOTT: Were you an English major in your undergraduate years at the University of Kansas? Were you writing poetry during those years?

STAFFORD: As an undergraduate I had majored in both English and economics, for I wanted to write but also wanted to help overcome the damage of the depression. My reading all slid toward literature, though, and I turned from the field of economics. My time in camp had confirmed in me the habit of daily writing; and in all the years since I have continued the habit. The result has been a torrent of manuscripts, many of them lurking in my attic, some fairly large number now published, poetry and prose.

ELLIOTT: You waited much longer than most poets feel they can wait to publish your first book of poetry. How do you feel about that?

STAFFORD: I was the first person in all the generations of my family to go to college, so I was not surprised about failing to publish early; and all my life I have felt lucky to find my way into print now and then. Through the very late 1940s and into the 1950s I had quite a few poems in periodicals; and by 1958 or so I circulated a collection but without any success. In 1960 my first collection came out, a small one called *West of Your City*. I was 36, but I didn't know any better—I thought I was quite headlong in my career.

ELLIOTT: You have been active in the Fellowship of Reconciliation. What exactly has been your role in that and similar organizations?

STAFFORD: Being a war resister, deliberately taking on the role of being different, permeated my life with an outsider attitude. In college I had engaged in sit-ins opposing segregation in the University of Kansas Union Building (which, like many other places, refused service to blacks). This was along in the late 1930s. We always felt that our stand then helped lead toward the later protests that caught the world's attention. In World War II some of us couldn't help feeling the irony of sending troops across the world to fight injustice when a black person would be denied fair treatment at home. So—I joined the War Resisters League and the Fellowship of Reconciliation. My wife and I have our 50-year certificate from the FOR, and our friends are largely associated with such organizations and movements. We have always assumed that such stands as we take may cost us, and in extreme instances (as in World War II for me) the cost may be significant. But generally we find ourselves and our views welcomed: I cherish the esteem of those around me, and voice my protest in such a way as to reconcile rather than to offend.

ELLIOTT: I have heard that one of your sons and his family are Quakers. Is that true?

STAFFORD: Yes, our children are of our persuasion.

ELLIOTT: In *Contemporary Authors* the first two items in your list of avocations are "Training children and dogs" and "pacifist organizations." I know you were being humorous in part, but if I can put those items together (leaving out the dogs), I'm wondering whether you feel that it is possible for parents to "train" their children to be pacifists.

STAFFORD: Train our children in our pacifist way? To us, conduct that leads to a good life and a fair attitude toward others is a natural way to live.

ELLIOTT: In what way might you see your poetry as being related to your lifelong commitment to peace?

STAFFORD: I suppose that the life of writing does conduce to sustained thinking and the consideration of consequences beyond the immediate and superficial. It is sort of like that question about why I worked. I thought every respectable person did. I still feel that way and look for goodwill and humanity everywhere, including among "the enemy."

ELLIOTT: Does the Quaker concept of the Inner Light have any active meaning for you in terms of creativity or how poetry comes out of meditation and quiet?

STAFFORD: For me, it's a handy phrase for something that I feel. It's not a matter of faith for me, but it is mysterious where things come from. I think this is true of many religious formulations. They are constructed in words that enable us to hold in mind, and work back and forth with, things that are in common for us, that are in common for us as human experience. And the Inner Light . . . I have some recent poems that haven't been published that are going to have a pretty close connection with what you're saying. One I almost read today. It says, "It is not by light and not by sound we find the truth, but inner light . . . ," I guess. It doesn't say inner light, but the idea is that something else needs to come and does come. Kind of a developing conviction that one has.

The following excerpt is from "Sharing Language: A Conversation with William Stafford," published in Teaching English in the Two-Year College, *December 1991.*

ELLIOTT: For some people you're one of the patron saints of process writing in composition classes, with regard to techniques for prewriting.

STAFFORD: All right!

ELLIOTT: In articles and textbooks, I've seen quotes from you about following whatever happens to come along in the writing process. And that's something we try to help our students with the most, to help them overcome writing blocks and the feeling that they can't get it out. People have found some of the things you say very useful because so often these days in teaching freshman composition we get students who just can't write. I don't mean not knowing the grammar, although that's certainly part of it. Are you aware of what I'm saying, that people claim you as an authority in composition classes? On the other hand, sometimes people say, "Isn't he primarily talking about writing poetry, or is he talking about something that would be true for freshman English with absolute beginners?"

STAFFORD: Everything. Now let me try to link together two things you said. You are too doctrinaire about people who can't write. Sure, everybody can write. I'm manifesting now what this is about: you just lower your standards and start there. So, when I'm teaching any group I naturally don't—but also by principle I don't—have standards. I am not disappointed in what someone says or writes because I'm not expecting anything except what comes. I'm just there, wherever it is. Sea level is where it is in this class, that's all. So, it's something I find in a class rather than having my idea of where it ought to be when I go in there; I just find it. That's part of it. I'll just make that little excursion.

Then to go back to what you said about being the patron saint or something of this process. I have, and I welcome in myself, just a childlike delight in what you say. I'm very glad to hear that, and I don't want to claim anything, but I will say—and I have said it when it was hard to say it, when I didn't do myself any good—I'll take my stand by that way of writing and teaching writing. Where it all came from, I don't know. I mean it may have had an other source, but it also sprang up wherever I was. It was just something that began to be *the way it is* for me, and I'm delighted to find (whoever the saint is) this process, or the recognition of making progress and doing art by acceptance and convergence—all these things. It's where I live.

ELLIOTT: I probably was too doctrinaire in saying that about students who can't write, but in a sense I was quoting what the students would say about themselves: "I can't write."

STAFFORD: I know they would. I wouldn't accept that.

ELLIOTT: I think your ideas help them cope with the feeling that they are tongue-tied, pen-tied, whatever you want to call it. I want to say to them, "Get it out; don't worry about it." But it took a long time before a number of composition teachers were able to accept that idea. It seemed too loose, too easy somehow.

STAFFORD: Maybe it is safer for me if I back up for a minute and say there are many people going around the country now with this process, exemplifying it. My hat is off to them, and when I meet them I feel convergent with them. Nobody is making any claims, but I just feel wholehearted allegiance. There are quite a number of them.

ELLIOTT: I was talking only a couple of days ago with people who were saying, "They've got to know the grammar before they can write." But if they are never going to write, what good is the grammar?

STAFFORD: Well, the awful thing is they know it. I mean grammar is what people use when they talk. I saw it defined a long time ago as the unconscious logic of the popular mind. To assume that mastery of punctuation, spelling, and how to avoid the more obvious of society's no-no's about the form of discourse will release students for a life of perfect talking and writing is nonsense, and dangerous nonsense. We have enough correct fools.

ELLIOTT: I have heard you say that you don't want to praise your students' writing. You don't want to disparage, but you don't want to praise either. But I often find myself dealing with students whose sense of written language is almost nonexistent. They really don't have any models that they have processed and which have become voices in their head that they can compare their writings to or get a sense of inspiration from. They are more an oral culture, and writing is something that has just not played much of a role in their lives. So when they make their achievements in writing, when they begin to do it, I always feel I want to encourage that along. But you have made me think twice. How would you deal with such students?

STAFFORD: Well, I feel easy about asserting something here. I don't want to push it; I want to put some "maybe" into this. But it seems easy to me in the real world to meet any student, no matter how afraid they are of writing, and if they write anything down I would look at what they have done as evidence (I don't know a better way to say this)—not as composition but as evidence of something that is happening with them and language. And I would not pat them on the head for this to encourage them (and if I could control my inner feelings, I would, and I think I can because I'm wholehearted about this) but I would respond to it. I mean I would indicate where I converged with what they had written; and maybe any remarks, either written or spoken, in the presence of what they have written, would be like "Kilroy was here" remarks to indicate that I was with them at this point, that I was following it. I mean I'm enigmatic about evaluation, just saying, "I was at that same corner that you're talking about," or "That's the building that such and such happened in." It indicates, "Yes, he did read it, but he didn't say good or bad." Sometimes I am not able to follow it, in which case I wouldn't hesitate to tell them I was not able to follow it. But I wouldn't ever try to tell them I couldn't follow it when I really could. And it's got to be really low if I can't understand it. I tell them things like, "I can understand the Rosetti Stone, no problem."

So, I think any student, any person talking or writing, is better served by attention and listening, reading and accompanying that person, than by being the machine in their presence who says "good" or "bad." I'm a human being. Is any person's writing utterly foreign to me? No, I've been there before, you know. It's not exactly understanding, it's not exactly trying to empathize, but it is sharing the experience of language.

I've never found anyone in actual life whose writing was just gibberish. You know, you said and we all say things like this—they really can't write well. If they come to college, they can probably draw out some words. They can draw out these words, and it's some words and not other words, and so I just begin to go into what words they are and what other words they aren't rather than encouraging them by saying "good." In some ways it's as easy as this: just be honest. My kind of honesty . . . I mean there is no problem for me, since I'm not expecting anything—I just have hopes. You could even indicate that to them and it wouldn't hurt them because they have already made that judgement that it's not good. So I don't disagree with them; I mean if they say it's no good, I see *how* it's no good, or something like that. Why did this go this way? Rather than "No" or "Yes," it is "Where?" "Tell me more," "Help me."

Maybe I can get the stance to take by citing this. A person told me years ago, "I talked to an editor and I said, 'When you get something that is really no good, what do you do?' This editor said, 'I ask myself what it is in me that is keeping me from perceiving what is in this particular work.'" I think that would be a helpful attitude to take. So, you see, there is evidence. I feel like a kind of super-Freud: "Does this have meaning?" Oh yes. More than you thought.

ELLIOT: But you were saying that when a student comes up to you and says, "Should I do it this way or this way?" you are very forthright in giving advice.

STAFFORD: I am forthright because then I know that we have converged where they are. They're ready for one or the other and they are really asking me something, which would not be demeaning of me. I would not demean them and I wouldn't assume any ignorance; I would just tell them what I feel. That's a wonderful place to be, and if they can get the feel of that for themselves, they shouldn't try to do any more than that. That's all there is in writing—this way or this way, rather than good or bad because good may be impossible, and bad is somebody else's judgement; it just happens to be where you are. So why not "this way or this way"?

ELLIOT: Could you say more about how students are harmed by evaluation and why they do not benefit from praise?

STAFFORD: If a student learns to seek praise and avoid blame, the actual feel and excitement of learning and accomplishing will be slighted in favor of someone else's reaction. The student's own, inner, self-realizing relation to the material is displaced. Anyone who customarily seeks outside rewards rather than inner satisfactions will be disabled, it seems to me, for all higher and original accomplishment. And that kind of teaching and "learning" will corrupt both student and teacher. For teachers will begin to feel themselves arbiters and guardians rather than participants in the excitement of skill and discovery.

ELLIOT: How do you cope with the demand for evaluation placed upon teachers by the education sytem, by administrators, or even by students?

STAFFORD: Once I took on the participating rather than the judging role, I had to be ready for reactions. And I was not heroic. If a student demands an evaluation, I give it; I cave in. And the same for a parent or administrator: I take whatever demands my bosses make (or change bosses, but that is difficult sometimes). My job, it seems to me, is to make clear what I think ought to be done. I can be overruled, and I let my preference be known. You might be surprised at how prevalently I was allowed my way. And even knowledge of what I wanted to do permeated the classroom: students knew I was on their side, on the side of experimentation, of worthy mistakes, of adventure rather than the trudging down established paths that most systems impose.

And let me put in that this nonevaluation impulse applies maybe with more force for beginners. Many teachers seem to think that students new to an endeavor require closely supervised training rather than the more free activity of those who have benefited from the teacher's guidance. Far from it, I say. If anything, the emphasis should be the other way around: beginners benefit from impulse, excitement, motion, trying out things without the menace of disapproval (or the distraction of imminent gaining of approval). The more advanced the student, the more able to take close, hovering, judgemental interchange.

I assume that there is no ceiling on one's education, that "accomplished" students are exalted only because they and their exalters are limited, that out there in the realm of our mutual seeking we all—students, teachers, and, yes, even our bosses—can continue to learn, without the distraction of pats on the head or raps on the knuckles. Education is too important and exciting to be dominated by thoughts of the hovering red pencil or the happy smiling face pasted in the margin.

III. Tracking the Mind

A Conversation with Robert Creeley

Scranton, Pennsylvania
April 1988

Robert Creeley (1926-2005) published his first book of poetry in 1952 and went on to publish over sixty more. His *Collected Poems* was published in two volumes appearing in 1982 and 2006. He taught at the University of Buffalo for many years and then at Brown University.

ELLIOTT: I'd like to start by talking to you about your relationship to jazz. You have sometimes referred to the influences of both jazz and abstract expressionist art on your poetry. Where do those two intersect for you?

CREELEY: I think in the sense of improvisation. Also the emphasis on feeling as a lead or a conductor, or a context in which to respond—how to articulate feeling. And then in either case the procedures, or what you did to have this possibility, were usually remarkably sophisticated. It never seemed to me that they were either crude or makeshift. I remember back in Black Mountain days that Stefan Wolpe, for example, felt that both Miles Davis and Charlie Parker were great musicians, and he was wanting to do a concetio or some such thing, for Charlie Parker in particular. He may have even done one. But he was fascinated by their authority as musicians. Very unlike Wynton Marsalis presently. That wasn't what he was talking about. That kind of pleasant popular rapport with the general public is certainly interesting, but it wasn't what he was meaning at all. These people were obviously geniuses.

ELLIOTT: I've been curious about one of your poems for years. Is "They" about free jazz?

CREELEY: Not specifically. As I look at it quickly, I think of Ed Dorn. There's a poem of his, when he's living in Santa Fe; it's in *The New American Poetry*. There's music in courts up the valley, and he hears this music. It's a sense of everyone has moved on. It's a classic nostalgic feeling of the late '50s, early '60s, that the people of one's heart are out there but the time has moved, the place and time have gone away, and "I wondered what had/ happened to the chords." By the time I get through with this poem, its "they" becomes the sense of all other people. You could think of "love, love, love" or something. It's like the Beatles, the '60s. But first the feeling to me is that nostalgia, what had happened to them, what happened to that place where other people were. I'm really responding to Ed's poem.

ELLIOTT: I was entirely wrong then with regard to your intention. It always struck me as a useful poem in terms of talking about what was going on in jazz starting in the '60s when chord changes had disappeared as such for many musicians of the avant-garde.

CREELEY: Yes, I hear. I'd happily listened a lot to Coltrane during the '50s. I can recall at the outset of the '50s there were two people among others who had a lot of authority—Sonny Rollins and Coltrane. And then Rollins didn't so much. He had that period where he didn't play for a while. And then Ornette Coleman became absolutely decisive. The first Coleman I heard I think was like late '50s. Not in person; it was always records at that time, very occasionally otherwise. But then I began to be fascinated by that whole imagination of how long can this particular moment be expanded. That was a fascinating premise. Cool jazz really bored me immensely, that sense of muting the kinds of intensity that were attractive to me.

Then of course we moved into the wild business of rock n' roll. That was fascinating! I remember, for example, being in San Francisco, in '65 or so. The Longshoreman's Hall, the Fillmore, and the Avalon, the three great communal places of dancing in San Francisco are now going full blast, and the Sopwith Camel, the Grateful Dead, and Big Brother and the Holding Company are all playing one night in the Fillmore, this long cavernous room, with Bill Graham's light show. We figured out that there were between two and three thousand people dancing that very night in that room. And if you took all the places where people were dancing in San Francisco, you'd come up with a number of about eight to ten thousand people dancing.

And that same time—it was that same week—John Coltrane was playing at the Jazz Workshop on Broadway, and Ornette Coleman was at another club just maybe a block up the street, and I went to hear Ornette Coleman. I think there were eight people. He was playing great. Eight people, like some wild stock movie number out of the '40s. I mean classic, very white girls with very black men, with immense black shades on. If you jingled change on the bar there would be this instant tension, and the music was very laid back. It was very good, but it was intensely self-conscious, intensely involved with the proper gestures. That is, the audience, not the musicians. So that was incredible.

And then I went up a night or two later to hear Coltrane, who had just opened, and that situation was very awkward. It was a long sort of channel-like seating. In other words, there was the bar as you came in, and it seemed you stepped down a couple of steps and went into a long narrow room, and the band was just at the end playing out to you. The sound was curiously lousy, but what was most awkward was that the racket from the bar action and then out to the tables was incessant, so finally I think after a day or two of that he just quit. I don't think anyone was listening at all the night I went.

60

ELLIOTT: More and more musicians at that time started giving up on clubs and saying they were just going to play concerts.

CREELEY: Yes, exactly. Or just forget it. This is awkwardly, presumptuously sociological, but jazz seems to have almost intently removed its audience. It certainly had come a long way from any active communal disposition. I love how LeRoi Jones, Amiri Baraka, has a really good point in *Blues People* when he's talking of the fact that the black musician (he uses in particular Louis Armstrong as instance) would be not just the emotional spokesman for the community, but that when he played, the community would have the tacit circumstance of celebration and communal gathering, that he would be a celebrant of that activity, one person used thus to collect people, to be a spokesman or center for that feeling, communally. He would therefore be a person entirely identified by the community, whereas the white musician (he uses, as a parallel, Bix Beiderbecke) would be a middle class drop-out trying to rebel against the mores and habits of the social group, and his playing music would be a rejection of those social dispositions. His mother and dad would not be down sitting at the club, or very rarely. He'd be rejecting the social group of which he was a member.

ELLIOTT: You were referring a few minutes ago to Coltrane and the idea of the extended statement. I just heard an anecdote in a video on Coltrane, where Elvin Jones was talking about how at times they would play sets that would last three hours. That sort of expansiveness started when Coltrane was with Miles Davis, and once Davis said, "How come you play such long solos?" Coltrane replied, "Well, sometimes I get started and I just don't know how to end it," and Davis said, "Take the horn out of your mouth."

CREELEY: The only other time I ever heard Coltrane play was just such an instance. He was playing with Thelonious Monk in New York and it was great, with Wilbur Ware on bass. I don't quite remember what they were playing, but I'll never forget the chorus, which was terrific. You could thankfully hear it because it was a small club. But they started and Thelonious Monk took a chorus. Then John Coltrane started and Monk was sort of backing him up for a while. Then he stops doing that and he goes to the men's room. I saw him in there briefly. Then he comes back, goes up to the bar, has a drink, talks to some friends, comes back and picks up. But it isn't indifferent. I mean Coltrane is still playing. It was a beautiful, incredible chorus. It's like, how do you get out of this? You can either stop, that's one solution, but that's cheating, so to speak. You have to come to that point where you can get off. Elvin Jones has a great sense of where you can get off.

ELLIOTT: I've been wondering about your relationship to jazz as it developed from the late '50s into the '60s, because it has always seemed to me that in cetiain ways the music of Coltrane in the mid-'60s and Coleman and Cecil Taylor and others had some parallels with much of the post WWII poetry you would align yourself with. When you get into the '60s, a rhythmic step beyond Elvin Jones occurs. Elvin Jones reached a point where he really couldn't play with Coltrane any more, or chose not to, and a new drummer took over. It was a freeing of jazz from the rigidity of the bar line in addition to freeing it from the chords. It seems to me, despite the influence of Parker and bebop on people like yourself, that jazz had been in a sense lagging behind what poets like you were doing rhythmically. And it wasn't until the '60s that in certain respects jazz became as free as poetry had been.

CREELEY: I remember Bob Callahan, who's a poet and publisher on the West Coast. One time I had a reading at St. Marks's, and afterwards he came out and said hello, and I realized the fellow with him was Cecil Taylor, who seemed to have liked it. That was fascinating. I found a really useful rapport with musicians of this particular music. It had nothing to do with content. That wasn't what they were hearing, and that's what I found was interesting. Way back, the people whom I'd really be picked up on by—that is, people in the usual audience, the ones who could, quote, "get it," who didn't see any problems, so to speak—were almost without exception musicians. Mathematicians never had any problems, or dancers —anyone who had either to do with duration or ways of measure, any system of measure that didn't have a necessary content that had to be "I love my mother" or "I'm a good person." They didn't want to hear aggressive, violent statements necessarily, but they certainly didn't worry about what was being said. They were fascinated by the system of the statement and how it worked as an effective system. I know Sheila Jordan, for instance, came generously to a reading not long ago and said, "It's like jazz," and I was very flattered.

I was fascinated by the agencies of stress and duration. That's what fascinated me with Parker initially, especially the numbers he played on the systems of time. I remember I had to share a place with a guy named Joe Laconi, who was going to the New England Conservatory of Music, and I was going to try to get myself to Harvard, so we shared this place on Tremont Street just around the corner from the Club Savoy and the Hi-Hat, where Serge Chaloff would be playing. Jackie Byard was the house piano for a long, long time.

Anyhow, we were there and Joe played trombone and I was supposed to learn bass and start playing with the group. But I remember playing records for Joe. Think of it—he was functionally a jazz musician with sophistication in training, but I remember playing to him things like "Chasin' the Bird," and he said, "They can't do that." I said, "What do you mean, they can't do that? You've got two periods and at the same time two figures. What's the problem?" He said, "No, no, that's not jazz; that's not the way to conceive of this activity; the time is wrong; there's no congruence." But to me . . . I mean it wasn't that I was brighter. In fact I was probably less trained, so there was no problem. But something as simple as that was confusing to him. Or when Charlie Parker, for example, would almost reverse time, turn around the beat and play it backwards. That's before you could do that on a tape recorder, so to speak. That was probably the first time I had ever heard of that sound. He would just play incredibly funny numbers on time. He was utterly witful of what he was doing.

The only time I heard him play, which was I would say less than a half a minute, he was to play at the Open Door or the Five Spot—I can't remember which—but Brew Moore was the house band, I thought a very sluggish musician and very dull. But anyhow, it used to be the battle of the saxes. So Charlie Parker was to come and play that evening, and a bunch of us all got there and got seats in this lounge-like cafe. And then Charlie Parker came on the stand with Brew Moore. They stated playing, and Brew Moore sort of began opening this song, playing the melody and what not, and the moment he got started Charlie Parker did that wild thing—he played through the melody at least double time, so just as Brew Moore was finishing it he'd come around and was back at the beginning and met him, almost like he drew a circle right around him figuratively, and then put down his sax and disappeared, just walked off the stage, not angry, just put it down and was off and didn't reappear all evening, until finally long after the audience was basically gone. It was myself and a friend having a late drink, and the door opens and he reappears, I remember his agent was there and says, "That was a really dumb thing you did." And Charlie Parker says, "Well, did you get the money?" And he says, "Yeah, I got the money, but they weren't happy. You got the crowd, but they didn't like that at all. But they did pay because you were here." Then he saw us sitting there and he said, "What are you people here for? What are you doing?" And I said, "We're here to hear you." He said, "Hah, good luck," and went off. That was it! So that was very interesting,

Thelonious Monk I thought was great, and Miles Davis. I loved it all. I loved Milt Jackson, and that was very easy for me to hear, that delayer [on the vibraphone] locating it, making a pattern of time, and making it specific to ways you felt in it. You know, in those days at least, it was a very established grid you were working on/with, so someone as myself without any particular training could certainly hear "I've Got Rhythm." I think of Eddie Berlin, a friend all my life, who was at that point friends with Dizzy Gillespie and Charlie Parker. He's really the person who first gives me records of all the 45's. The first one I remember distinctly is "Now's the Time/Billie's Bounce," the single, and then it goes on and then it goes sort of backwards and forwards.

I had a friend in college named Herbie Cole, who had a classic record collection, back to New Orleans jazz. All the classic stuff—Mugsy Spanier and Kansas City and New Orleans and Chicago and up to bands of that time. But he stopped short of, as I remember, Lester Young, or just on the other side. And then my friends in college really liked Chu Berry and Ben Webster very much. They liked the sound, and Coleman Hawkins albums. Buddy played saxophone and Rice was a piano player. My friend named Joe Leach, who'd come from Detroit, already was playing with Howard McGhee and Milt Jackson, had gone to the high school with them and played professionally with them. His family were old time vaudeville people who had started a chain of drugstores and became successful. They wanted to get their son out of the world of show biz, so they got him to Harvard. I remember—it was very dazzling to us—*Down Beat* had a little note saying, "Boston jazz aficionados will be pleased to know that Joe Leach will be now in Boston." He was a very good friend, lives now in California.

ELLIOTT: In John Wilson's preface to the collection of essays about your work that he edited [*Robert Creeley's Life and Work: A Sense of Increment*] he stressed something that I had thought about your poetry too, that of all the modern jazz musicians Monk seems to be the one that is somehow most in affinity with what you're doing rhythmically—sort of fragmentation and delaying of accents.

CREELEY: There's a sweet man in Boston, from Belmont, Pancho Savery, who wrote a piece, a very charming parallel between Thelonious Monk and my interests as a poet where he's making kind of a playful comparison—hats, for example, things of that kind.

ELLIOTT: You mentioned Sheila Jordan. *Down Beat* gave a Blindfold Test to her a few years ago. As you probably know, what they usually do is if they have a vocalist as the subject they'll play vocalists for her to identify; if they have a trombonist they'll play trombonists and so on. So they were playing vocalists and she was commenting about people like Ella Fitzgerald. Then they threw her a poem by you. She had never heard you read, and she said, "Oh, that must be Robert Creeley." This was after she'd done the album with Steve Swallow [*Home: Music by Steve Swallow to Poems by Robert Creeley*].

CREELEY: That's really great. She's an extremely dear person.

ELLIOTT: What was your reaction to Swallow's record?

CREELEY: I was dazzled and pleased. When we lived in Bolinas, Steve Swallow and his wife and children were living just at the head of the road we lived on, Terrace Avenue. It was a short road, and it was dramatically called "the edge of the sea." We lived about two-thirds of the way up, and Steve rented a house just at the head of the street. He was good friends with Ebbe Borregaard. His wife was a very interesting, pleasant woman. She was working as a nurse in Point Reyes, particularly involved with the clinic there that was interested to emphasize the communal, and practicality, and the human pleasure of home births—you know, go back to midwifery. At that time, the whole imagination of the town was to do it yourself, the communal support. So she was working very much in that interest.

And Steve, whom I knew of but not really well, was described to me as this really incredible jazz bassist who chose to live out there. He's not shy, but he goes about his own business, quiet, and so Ebbe, I think, was the only friend that ever saw much of him. Ebbe later told me it was fascinating talking to him about music and ways you might hear things, try this, try that. I always felt friendly toward him. We would see each other, wave and say hello as neighbors. But I never had the chance to talk to him. So he would pick up jobs as groups came into San Francisco wanting an active bass player, and they'd always get him. And then I guess he decided it was getting too restrictive, because he couldn't just hang out and he never really had enough decision about whom he worked with.

So they determined to go back to the East Coast. They got a place in Connecticut, Guilford, and then I didn't hear from him for a while. He'd gone back working in New York, and then I got out of the blue a letter from him saying he'd done settings, as he put it, or compositions for some ten poems of mine, and there was now a chance to record them and would I mind, would I feel that was agreeable. And I thought, "Wow, terrific!" He was inmensely fair. He meticulously set it up, got me enrolled in B.M.I., etc. He handled that whole business with impeccable clarity, so that for the first couple of years of the album's publication you certainly got a substantial feedback from it, payment of royalties on it, and very fairly dealt with. So I was fascinated. We were living in New Mexico when I actually heard the first track taped. And it took me a while to get located. I mean bebop is not Steve's favorite music. To him it would be like New Orleans to someone who was interested in bebop. It's like, "Come on, give us a break, we've heard that stuff until it's coming out our ears." He gets very bored with it as a structure, so he wasn't interested much in that at all.

So when Steve told me about the first recording session, he said it went absolutely great. They did just one take and everybody agreed it was just terrific and that was it. So they went home with this great elation and he gets home and there's a letter from his wife saying, "I'm leaving you." Wouldn't you know it, after a day of recording Robert Creeley you'd have a note like that. It sort of figured. [Laughing]

Then the other record, the Steve Lacy [*Futurities*]—that was very curious how that happened. I'd known of Steve Lacy I think with Cecil Taylor. The record of his I first really heard was the one that has "Easy to Love" on it. It was his first group, mid to late '50s, and he was beginning to play Thelonious Monk.

Then I sort of lost track of him [Lacy]. Occasionally friends would show me records. I knew he was living in France, but some couple of years ago, three or four at least, thanks to an editor of a magazine called *Entre Tien* that did a number on Williams, and a number on Beat writers or Projectivists, I got a reading in Paris, two very excellent readings, one at the Pompidou Center and the other at the museum, so these were very auspicious and active readings, with a great bunch of translators and what not. This editor also had a spot on Radio France called "The Wings of the Albatross." He asked me if I would mind doing an interview. I said terrific. Then low and behold, when I arrived in Paris there was Pierre Joris, a poet who had a magazine called *Six Pack* that did a beautiful sort of elegy issue for Paul Blackburn when he sadly died, and I knew his poetry and we had many friends in common. This other fellow, the editor, wanted to have it be a casual interview, so they'd been talking in the car, sort of *cinema verite* mode, lots of traffic noises, talking. They got talking about my poetry to the extent that they made me wait 20 minutes while they continued their conversation. But anyhow, as we were coming into the city, they said they knew my interest in jazz and therefore they were trying to find some situation or contact locally that could make a decor for that interest, make a context for it. So Pierre said, "Well, we thought of Steve Lacy." I said "Steve Lacy?" And he said, "Yes, he's a friend who lives just around here. He'd be pleased to say hello." I said I'd be pleased to say hello to him.

So up we went and I liked him on the instant and also Irene Aebi. She was great. It turned out Irene was the classic Swiss kid. She had had a great ambition in her youth to get to San Francisco and hang out with the Beats. So she got there, but she got there late. She connected with Jack Spicer and that whole scene, so she had this remarkable lore. I mean she knew all of my friends from that particular world, and she's incredibly literate and bright, good natured person. And then Steve—I had always imagined Steve (again, white man's burden) as some really swinging black man. No way, he's a Russian Jew. So I had had the wrong ethnic identity entirely. It turns out he was close friends of Larry Fagin. He knew Anne Waldman. There was a lot of interrelation.

And so he came to the reading that night. He did some improvising back of me that was kind of good-natured patience for the radio interest. The talking was very fine and good. I felt very at home with him. So he came that night and Brion Gysin, who was still alive and who was a friend of his, he came. Julian Beck was there. It was an incredible evening. As we were leaving we talked a bit about keeping in touch, and he said, "Would you mind if I tried a setting of that poem you read, 'The Rhythm'? If you could get me a text of that I'd be fascinated to try to do something." I said, "Yeah!" I was glad there was an interest. I sent him a book or two and I got back home, and again all was quiet, and that's fine.

Then suddenly comes this incredible notebook. I don't know if you've ever seen his final scores. They're incredible. He puts in little pictures and dedicates each piece to a particular artist or a hero of imagination, like Leonardo Da Vinci or whomever; it's just very very funny and terrific. So then the whole project got more and more vast. I mean first he was going to do one poem. Now he's done twenty poems and he's imagining a whole musical. And it has two dancers—Douglas Dunn, this extraordinary dancer from New York, and also an African woman, Elsa Wolliastone. So they are the dancers, not opposed but quite different. She's a big, hefty woman and he's a very lithe and slender man. So it was a very curious complement. They did the whole dance thing. And then Steve had a backdrop with a Ken Noland, a big Ken Noland triangle. They put it on in France, Italy, Switzerland, and England. I bleakly never got a chance to see it. I was trying to contrive to get over there. It came out in that two record set you probably know. It isn't Steve's responsibility or fault, but I've gotten one copy of the record I think that he sent me and that's about it.

ELLIOTT: To my ear, Sheila Jordan's voice seemed more compatible with . . .

CREELEY: Irene Aebi did it as a classic like *Sprechstimme*.

ELLIOTT: Somewhat strident.

CREELEY: Yes, strident and deliberate. But I think that Steve Lacy's take on it is very both legitimate and canny. The thing that really gets to me in Steve Swallow's, in Sheila Jordan's singing, is the extraordinary accuracy of the hearing. I mean the way she sings, for example, "Nowhere one / goes will / one ever / be away / enough from / wherever one was." The way she sings through that and hears the pattern of the sound is just . . . I mean how Steve wrote it. So that's delicious to have someone hear it that specifically. The other record is very different, although "Mind's Heart," that particular take, is really extraordinary. They certainly got that one. The music on it I enjoy.

ELLIOTT: I have a lot of respect for Lacy's music. He's a wonderful original.

CREELEY: I do too. He's really tough. He stays put.

ELLIOTT: I'm interested in what you said about the Steve Swallow song. One thing associated with your way of reading your poetry is the pause at the end of each line. Neither of the Steves nor of the vocalists does that.

CREELEY: Except for Sheila in that one, but mostly not.

ELLIOTT: Mostly not in others. I was wondering if you felt it was a valid approach, even though you wouldn't score it that way if you were reading it.

CREELEY: Steve Swallow said, after it was all done, that what he wanted was to let the poem, either at the beginning or the end of the activity, set and/or reflect on or qualify—be the sponsoring agency of—what either followed or preceded, so that it would set a thing in mind or a context. So I figured that's the case. No, I can't dictate the terms of how it's read more than the typography permits. If the typography doesn't do it then I don't know what will. "I wondered what had / happened to the chords. / There was a music, // they were following / a pattern. It was / an intention perhaps." [Reading a portion of "They"] I can hear that easily. I mean I can hear that as a pattern without any problems. I think probably Steve Swallow heard the rhythmic patterns more sensitively. He just heard my sense of them more particularly than did Steve Lacy. Steve Lacy was using them almost like kind of dramas, using them in a more melodramatic way. He's more interested in the subjects really. I don't think Steve Swallow was. He was, but not really.

ELLIOTT: The selection of poems reflected that difference.

CREELEY: Exactly.

ELLIOTT: I thought much of the success of Swallow's record was because of Sheila Jordan. She really seemed to me to get the tone of your poetry well. I also thought that on Swallow's record the melodic intervals and so on seemed very compatible with your poetry. I mean, if he wasn't getting the exact rhythmic feel that you get out of reading, the melodic contours were very compatible.

CREELEY: Absolutely, and the feeling he certainly gets incredibly. He sure knows what I'm talking about, and he knows what's important to me to get located. I wish selfishly I had more contact with him, but I really don't. I mean I know where he is, but he's on the road.

ELLIOTT: On the subject of the way you read, in an essay by Bob Hass . . .

CREELEY: An old colleague from Buffalo.

ELLIOTT: He talks about how someone has reported that you just assumed William Carlos Williams read his poetry with pauses at line breaks, apparently because of how it looked on the page, without having . . .

CREELEY: That's true, because I was pretty displaced when I realized that neither he nor Zukofsky, those two poets who are crucial to me, seems to make a distinct . . . Louis reads right through line endings. I don't think I rarely if ever recall anything where they are crucial as a pivot. Williams was ambivalent, because there's a poem of his that I remember well from an early record published by the National Council of Teachers of English. It had on it, for example, the poem "The Wind Increases": "The harried / earth is swept / . . . / the tulip's bright / tips / sidle and / toss—" etc. etc. In that poem at least, if one takes the reading and puts it in context together with the text, there seems to be a pretty solid congruence of pacing according to the line endings and all, so the whole mode of the poem is explosive and emphatic. You know, "The Wind Increases"! Exclamation point! "The harried / earth is swept / . . . / the tulip's bright / tips / sidle and / toss . . . " I was fascinated by the way the breaks there seem to give it information. And then there's another poem of his, a very simple one: "Liquor and love / when the mind is dull / focus the wit / on a world of form . . . " ["The World Narrowed to a Point"]. In the second verse (there are only three verses, quatrains) there's the phrase, "inflections / ride the quick ear." I was fascinated by the way the word "inflections" and the rhythm of that word play on the base of the rhythm and shift the whole sense of duration. But as I say, I was disappointed that Williams, at least in my understanding, didn't seem to employ the line endings in quite the way I had anticipated.

Despite all the intensive writing on senses of measure and metric, I think the most articulate piece by Williams I know is still that very early one. I want to say the late teens maybe. I can't recall the title of the piece, but it has particularly to do with rhythm, and it's a very clear sense of cadence or how one measures in relation to rhythm and time. Otherwise, there is a letter to Eberhhart where he's talking about the base of the prosody, what he's calling the variable foot, and that's sort of interesting. It isn't that his metric is hard. I mean you can feel it and get hold of it quite simply, but trying to spell it out for friends or students is awful because it doesn't have any reality for them. It's all so arbitrary, they think.

ELLIOTT: Hass speculates that Williams's line endings were more for speed and to keep it going.

CREELEY: Yes. Mine are pivots. They give me a way to ground and/or locate a rhythmic base.

ELLIOTT: One of the things that is sometimes said about metrical verse, in which you can see an analogy to music, is that the way a phrase goes over from one line to the next is sort of like a musician's phrasing over the bar line.

CREELEY: Yes, right.

ELLIOTT: In a sense you subvert that.

CREELEY: Yes, I hear you.

ELLIOTT: The syntax of a sentence goes over the pauses, but the pauses are creating, again, more Monk-like rhythmic units.

CREELEY: It almost becomes a parody of the metronome. I mean the beat is paradoxically more determining than the syntax, and that's what I love, the fact that the rhythm becomes an expressiveness equal to that of the statement.

I remember Robert Duncan . . . I had been reading quite a bit publicly, and I was complaining that I was really getting bored of my own writings. I was having to mouth it over and over. And then he said, "Well, why don't you read for a different action? Read it one night for the thing you are saying, but then read it just for the rhythms. Forget what else . . . " And it was immensely useful. I realized I could read it a long time just as rhythmic structure, and whether people cried or laughed, I didn't really care or listen.

ELLIOTT: I'd like to move on to another area. The title of your most recent book is *Memory Gardens*, but you have passages in earlier poems and essays that are speaking against memory so to speak, and now there's so much of that in the recent poetry, the last three books really.

CREELEY: Well, it's age, obviously. I think of memory as kind of an accomplishment, a renewal, so that I don't feel in some agony of displacement that I could not have anticipated the prospect or fact of age as it proves to be. It's a new place, so the ways I felt about the world and myself in it in the, say, ages middle or late twenties through forties, are much changed at present. I think that's true. Memory becomes a mind function that is very, if not freaky, then curiously phenomenal in age, for many reasons. I mean the brain function begins to shift or to alter. Memory is not really dependable. It isn't something as dramatically displacing as Alzheimer's, gratefully, but it's a very funny circumstance to realize that memory is now constituting almost an equal time with reality, and that memory is now beginning to prove not a unifying disposition of world but a paradoxically isolating one. Take a song like "I Remember You." That's the classic human address to memory. I remember all the people who put me in this place. It's curious to realize you're remembering things that no one else remembers and you're not sure that you remember them either. It's a very funny human place to be. Nostalgia is very destructive, as with sentimentality. I like those two emotions, but I've never known how to propose them as public value without getting booed off the stage. I mean everyone seemingly has them.

The poets I find now probably as most active company to my own states of mind are Robert Duncan and John Ashbery. Really despite Robert's having died in February, he still stays immensely close to my heart, but also to my ways of thinking. For a long time in our lives he's been very useful precedence for human life and real body. He was about seven years older, so he would always be just a phase ahead of me, so I could actually ask him what's it like and get an accurate and clear answer. Those poems in the last two books are incredibly articulate about senses of how death is humanly. I think they're incredible poems of that experience.

And the other poet I feel very close to in terms of what's in mind is John Ashbery. Really I must say he's getting to be closer and closer. I mean I had a time when I respected his poetry and even thought I liked it, but I didn't really hang out with it very much. Then I went back to the book that's really crucial for me, his *Three Poems*. I remember Bill Berkson, who was a neighbor in Bolinas, had "The New Spirit." He had the manuscript, much of the book, from John, and I remember he gave me "The New Spirit" to look through, and I thought it was kind of interesting, but I came to like it very much, and then I read the *Self Portrait in a Convex Mirror* that got happily such public approval. That was good natured and easy stuff. I like very much his recent book, *April Galleons*. He's involved with a work that's very parallel to the one I'm interested in. What does one know of memory until there's an adamant need or occasion for it? Otherwise memory's a bore. I remember, for example, I used *Three Poems* in teaching. I had to realize that here I was with a group of people, age 20-25, to whom that poem was a vast and insistent bore. You know, what does he mean he doesn't know who he is, or he's momently some place but what he presumes to be there is now dissipated? Forget it! How could he even remember where he parked the car? I thought how it's a very peculiar feeling, but this man is making it extremely articulate. But, sadly, for the social needs there's little interest in knowing about that.

ELLIOTT: I read a review of *Mirrors* . . .

CREELEY: I liked *Mirrors* a lot.

ELLIOTT: Yes, I do too, but this reviewer almost felt as if you had betrayed your earlier principles. But it seems to me that the point of intersection with your early work, or rather the reason why there is no divergence, is because it's not so much memory per se but attention to the mind in the act of memory.

CREELEY: Yes, thank you, because that would be my defense, that what one's trying to do is to stay in the attention that the mind permits. Tracking the mind is really where it's at, if you can track the mind with the mind, which seems a contradiction in possibility. That's what's interesting to me. I'd go anywhere it takes me, because I don't see where else would I go. I mean there are attitudes and commitments I hope to feel forever.

Penelope, my wife, says, "Watch out for the graveyard shift." The way the whole prospect of statement or address becomes just the sense that everything's going. I think that takes care of itself. I've been working more recently in different guises and ways.

I would like to become almost more clichéd, not in the sense of popular, but in the sense of becoming accessible. I've always loved clichés. I think that's what is interesting in Ashbery's writing. He is the master of cliché—a genius, and very funny. Clichés are endlessly droll and productive and interesting, so I would like to write a poetry that became less singularly invested and more commonly stated. By "common" I mean simply a diction common to usual understanding and use. But again, that's something I can't dictate entirely at all.

I thought at one time two things that I'd love to do would be to write a sequence of poems which were based on what I could remember of interesting poems I have or haven't read in the past, not as jokes but just an attempt to make a poem of my own memory of these virtues of the poem that I . . . I realized for years I misquoted poems of Hart Crane's. My quote was, "Square sheets they saw the marble into there at the island quarry." I looked at the poem ["Island Quarry"] in the last year or so and I realized there are at lest two more syllables in that line, at least, and I've compacted it. Or I remember once way back in school days when I was asked to memorize a poem and write it down for the class—you know, that old-fashioned scene. I must have been a junior in high school, and I memorized Emily Dickinson's "Inebriate of air am I." So I came in and wrote it down, and I remember the teacher, a pleasant man, said, "How in the name of heaven could you misquote that line?" And I thought, "What have I done?" "Instead of saying, 'Inebriate of air am I,' you say, 'I am an inebriate of air.'" It just shifts the whole modality and the rhythms again. Why is it those rhythms so change when you say it that way? That's fascinating. I couldn't say, "Inebriate of air am I." No one in my world said things like that. I just didn't feel the confidence to say it that way.

And then I'd like to translate. I did once in *Presences*. There's a section of the one on the Dane and the castle. It's approximate translations of material coming from a catalog on Marisol's work that was published in Venezuela, so I would just grab what looked to be melodramatic phrases, like "sunglasses" or something. They're describing the pieces and talking about the effects of the physical appearances of these images, but I frankly don't know Spanish. I don't have any Spanish dictionary and I'm sort of winging it. When I don't know a word I just put something in. It seems immensely irresponsible, but it's a lot of fun. It's a source, a source for doing something.

ELLIOTT: I came across an interview where you were telling someone (this was back in the early '70s, I guess, maybe just after *In London* or around that time) that you were going through a period where poetry didn't seem very productive for you.

CREELEY: Yes, well I think Charles Bernstein said something yesterday that really had a lot of resonance. He said that he had happily met Carl Rakosi in the last couple weeks. He was amazed that this man now in his 80's was so articulate. It was a very pleasant meeting. In talking he had to realize that Carl Rakosi had a lot of questions about Louis Zukofsky's work, which I think is Charles Bernstein's interest in the same way that it is for me. He

74

thinks a lot of it. He also thinks a lot of Rakosi and Oppen and Reznikoff, the whole cluster. But I think Louis is the most intellectually provocative to him as a writer. But in any case, Carl was saying he found it questionable that Zukofsky had seemingly these intensive ellipses in his writing that were very awkward for the reader because he/she was suddenly stuck with a gap. To which Charles replied (no aggression): "Well, think of it. You're writing and something thus can't be brought together in a way that makes an accessible continuity, and ellipsis is all you've got as an agency." He said he found if one were thinking of ellipses, to him the much more dramatic instance would be the fact that neither Rakosi nor Oppen was able to write for about 20 or 30 years on the basis of political/social preoccupation. Now that is a very big blank for the reader, so that Zukofsky's determination to be able to continue writing, with or without the coherences that Carl might think requisite, is finally more interesting than saying nothing for 20 years. I wonder what Carl says of that. It was a very curious point.

The thing is that if one is not so much committed to writing as though taking a pledge, but if writing is one's delight and means of doing something, should I say, then truly one wants as much provocation of its activity as one can get. I remember it's like Ted Berrigan used to say—"There's no such thing as a bad book." He loved to read, and he was in some respects indifferent to what was given him to read. He was one of those readers who would literally finish one book, put it down, and pick up another. Anything that had a narrative, anything that went on, he would read. I think that's really true. Anything that permitted him to read, he would read. And the parallel, for example, is the great story about, I think, Trollope, who would, let's say, finish a novel at eleven in the morning and start another by three in the afternoon. My kind of writer! I mean, I was fascinated to be a writer of that order. I've had respect for people who are intensive journalists, who weren't writing for more than the effect of the day—a day's experience is what could be said. To me in poetry I'm certainly engaged and interested deeply by that which permits me to do this.

I think one factor of aging is that the expectable stimuli during, say, times of one's youth and/or middle age—emotional shifts, states, and so on—no longer become intensive provocation that they had been, so they don't frankly serve as the, quote, "impulse" quite so either dependably or in fact. Now emotion is more complex, not so much one's to be wary of it. It's more complex in its relationship. One wants to be tied into the communal as much as possible because that's something that tends to dry up. I think children and old folks need community, not just to help them across the street but because it's a situation that they really need. Whereas adults can possibly live in deserts or tops of mountains and otherwise and get on for a while. I think age and childhood really require the species—you know, collectively—rather than some isolated determinant. I think in one sense the provocations for an art come largely from that. Either that or a comfortable obsession, like Turner's, or Yeats's possibly, or Williams's. Williams was obviously absolutely intent upon getting something together, which was frustrating. It seems to have given him a base for writing right up to the end. Robert had a kind of grand design, as did Pound and Louis have a grand design. Louis had a project for each decade of his life. Remember, he finishes A, and then the next project in the '60s is the sequence involving flowers, but then trees would have been the next decade's prospect. He began them and then died in '72 or '73. So I think that would be immensely useful. I think one gets over the drama of one's own life as a singular value. Like I see ourselves more and more as I used to see chickens—terrific, but, you know, expectable.

ELLIOTT: Getting back to music for a minute . . . During all the phases of your career, the thing that holds everything together for me in terms of my interest is ultimately the rhythm.

CREELEY: Yes—"It is all a rhythm." I sure think so. I was thinking yesterday: in this undergraduate class I teach we've come pretty much to the end of the reading I'd thought to do. There's one more book, but it's a collection of critical articles, basically a vocabulary rather than a content I wanted to consider. So I'm trying to think of things that I can use as material to keep the center, and I was just walking . . . Buffalo, the campus, is very, very awkward. It's a sprawling campus, very decentralized. Because of the weather there are these long walkways between buildings, second floor tunnel-like walkways. And so I walk to the building that is the English department's location through at least three or possibly four other of these buildings, then through this long tunnel which is a communal walkway. I thought of taking a tape recorder and just hearing the rhythm of people saying things as I go along. It's terrific! I don't want to get too cozy or too cutsie about it, but just walking over it could really be interesting to hear what you hear. Try to think is there any point to it. I mean, people talking about lunch or I'll see you later or the world's ending. It's the rhythm, as you say, that's really interesting.

Notes

Creeley, Robert. *The Collected Poems of Robert Creeley, 1945–1975.*
      Berkeley: University of California Press, 1982.
Lacy, Steve. *Futurities: 20 Poems From Robert Creeley.* hat ART. 1989. CD.
Swallow, Steve. *Home: Music by Steve Swallow to Poems by Robert*
      Creeley. ECM. 1980. CD.
Williams, William Carlos. *The Collected Poems of William Carlos Williams,*
      Volume 1, 1909–1939. New York: New Directions, 1986.
_____. *The Collected Poems of William Carlos Williams, Volume 2, 1939–*
      1962. New York: New Directions, 1986.
Wilson, John, ed. *Robert Creeley's Life and Work: A Sense of Increment.*
      Ann Arbor, MI: University of Michigan Press, 1987.

IV. A Struggle Between Silence and Words

A Conversation with David Ray

Scranton, Pennsylvania
April 1991

David Ray (b. 1932) has written poetry, fiction, essays, and memoir. *Music of Time: Selected and New Poems* was published in 2006. He taught at the University of Missouri–Kansas City and elsewhere, in this country and abroad.

ELLIOTT: What I'd like to discuss with you is the relationship between your poetry and political or social issues, but before talking about *this* country, I'd like to ask how your experiences living in other countries might have modified your view of the United States. So many of your poems, and really the whole of *The Maharani's New Wall*, deal with travel.

RAY: That's sort of an accident in the sense that I've lived in a lot of different places, but basically I've very quickly established the same rut wherever I've been. I mean I get into a sort of ritualized observance of the day and it doesn't matter much. We've really lived pretty much the same kind of life in several different countries and we're still doing that. We're going to Australia in the fall, and we'll be out there for several months. I won't say I've not suffered culture shock, because I have, and I've gotten homesick at times in other countries, but I go through that kind of experience in the States too. To me this is and always has been the strangest country there is, and it remains very strange to me—almost as fragmented and vibrant in its way as India. People are wearing T-shirts now that are made out of cut-out flags, and a year ago you could have gotten arrested for that. You know, that was desecration of the flag and now it's this wave of patriotism that's supposed to guarantee another four years for George Bush. So the views of experience are strangely different. Is that honoring the flag or is it desecrating it? Maybe it depends on who's wearing the T-shirt. Can you imagine the police state walking up to find out what the motive is? Are you wearing this cut-out flag T-shirt in order to honor the flag or to desecrate it? If you give the wrong answer, then off you go—up against the wall or into the cell for reprogramming.

ELLIOTT: It's a very bizarre commentary on the First Amendment.

RAY: You see, if I were programmatic in my work I would also be programmatic about what I notice and what I write about. But that's come up again and again—"How could you let politics enter your work?" Well, how can you keep it out of your work? How can you control your *donné*, as James would say. How can you pre-filter your impressions or your feelings? I try to be as open as I can, and that means a certain vulnerability. That's always the case, and I don't know how to get around that because I'm not really willing to draw that frame tighter—on either my experience or my work.

ELLIOTT: With your involvement in the Poets Against the Vietnam War as a background, do you feel that a significantly smaller number of poets see a public role for poetry today? And what effect do you think the war in the Persian Gulf might have on the situation?

RAY: Okay, I've written quite a number of poems about this recent mess and my feeling about them is that these poems are unpublishable. It's what Solzhenitsyn said when he came to the States 15 to 20 years ago. He said he very quickly discerned something about this country, which was that censorship is just as pervasive here as it is in Russia. He said the difference is simply that its effect is felt in not so blunt a way; if you say something unpopular or unorthodox here, you can't get it published. And I believe that's basically true. If you can get it published, it will be ignored. So I think there are people with all kinds of things to contribute to society who are just ignored. And the current fashions in poetry, of course, are dictated by critics like the one who recently, for the first time in my awareness, used the adjective "ethical" as a put-down term of contempt and scorn, a very influential critic who has put down content basically. It's this old war that has gone on in the arts for a long time, and the current fashion, of course, is very much for what this critic calls "transcendent meditation," meaning work that is so personal as to be obscure, so private and hermetic as to be almost completely opaque to the reader without a great deal of study and the help of critics like herself. There's a very high premium on obscurity, of course, because it gives full employment to such critics. But let's say you happen to be one of those proletarians who writes relatively realistic, narrative-line autobiographical work—the roving reporter of poetry in a sense—poems of ethical concern, political poems, if you will. Can you see that work being published in *The New Yorker*?

So there's a very odd thing, and this was true of the Vietnam War and is true today: If as a future archaeologist you were to search through cultural artifacts for references to what was going on in the real world, you wouldn't find much in the poetry. Now what academics do is polarize everything, and they say, "You're advocating shrillness; you're advocating politics instead of poetry." Not at all! I'm saying that issues in life should also be issues in poetry. It's not a matter of "ought." If I cannot express my passionate concerns, then why would I be writing? I can't understand people who write without having passionate concerns to express, and I can't compartmentalize my own nicely into those that fit my aesthetic and others that don't.

ELLIOTT: This recent war had an air of surreality to me. It was almost like the war that didn't happen. It was over so quickly and there was such an effective effort on the part of the government (and the people and the media fell right into it) to manage the news and squelch all dissent, unlike the great amount of dissent that was in the air during the Vietnam War.

RAY: Right. It was the most effective use of propaganda since. . . Well, you know, we can fill that in later. I'm not aware that propaganda has ever been used that effectively for a fairly anomalous cause. Maybe it was used effectively in World War II or the Korean War. I don't know. What the Iraqis were doing in Kuwait was certainly bad, and certainly action needed to be taken, but the incredible self-righteous outrage of Bush, and the strange mission of killing over 100,000 people in order to protect 750,000. And stirring that pot of suffering and then turning around and saying, "Well it's none of our business."

I have a poem called "Armageddon." It is an example of a poem expressing this kind of concern—a genre, in other words, that I consider virtually unpublishable. I woke up one morning thinking, we are always anticipating the battle of Armageddon, but what if we have already had the battle of Armageddon and we don't know it? After all, we have these 600 oil wells blackening the sky; we have bombed Iraq back to the pre-industrial age; we are condoning this fantastic suffering that is going on there now. Even as we talk, last night [April 16, 1991] hundreds of people died of exposure and starvation in those mountains in northern Iraq and we turn our back. As e.e. cummings said in his poem about the Hungarian Revolution in 1956, "Uncle Sam shrugged a liberal titty and winked in the other direction." Something like that; that's not an exact quote. Eisenhower had told the Hungarians, "Rise up and we will help you." So they rose up and then a little while later the Soviets were using *Life* magazine pictures to identify the kids they were stringing up from lampposts.

So here too we have this business of Bush encouraging change, and then saying when help is really needed by the Kurds, "Well, we helped Kuwait because of some technicality that you don't qualify for. You're not qualified for our help." I think, though, that if someone were to take strong leadership and start to give some moral instruction to the country, the country might be more responsive. It's just that everybody is so cowardly—those spineless Congressmen who just fall into line. And on the war issue, even those who spoke out against the war, as soon as the decision was made, said, "Oh well, now that the decision is made . . . " As if convictions were for throwing away as soon as the majority outvotes you.

ELLIOTT: Getting back to the question of travel. The entirety of *The Maharani's New Wall* is about your experiences in India. Compared to some of those other places that you have written about, was there something about India that was more compelling? The obvious thing is your concern for poverty, which simply can't be ignored there. I heard someone who went to India say that the only things there are birth and death.

RAY: It's rather mind-boggling to realize that since we were there in 1982 they have added upwards of 165,000,000 people to their population, *our* population in that amount of time. If we went there now it would be vastly more overcrowded than it was eight years ago. When we were there, Calcutta, Bombay, and New Delhi were the really terrible cities, but forecasts are for having sixty cities like that by the year 2000, and by that I mean cities that are totally unmanageable in terms of basic human services.

ELLIOTT: In the poem, "Mammalapuram," you imply that the lesson of seeing that kind of poverty is one you felt your daughters needed; and presumably it would seem by extension that it is a lesson for all of us.

RAY: This is very relevant to what we were saying about Iraq. Where is any feeling for those Kurdish people? When I look at pictures of them, they look like *family*. I mean they look like terrific people. But we don't care enough even to use *words* as protection for them. We don't care whether they are gunned down from helicopters. I must say we haven't traveled very far since Vietnam if that's all the concern we have for these people. They called Asians "gooks" and didn't think of them as people, fired on them at random; and they don't seem to think Kurds are people either. I don't think the American people have yet come to the realization that as a result of that vote in Congress (which worked out one way instead of another because some people didn't speak up quite as strongly as they should have) we killed 100,000 people or more, and people will be dying for years to come because of this operation. They left mines and shells everywhere all through the desert, and we are still getting casualties from

84

the Vietnam War from mines and weapons left behind. How extensive can denial go? We deny the consequence of our own power.

ELLIOTT: For me the central poem in the book is the title poem, with that image of the Maharani building a wall to shut off the view of those peasants.

RAY: I saw her—the Maharani—as a kind of a witch figure. No, she didn't care about them. And the wealth that was coming out of that country was being sent in gold bullion bars to Swiss banks—incredible corruption. Ironically, some Indian writers are just now getting around to writing about the corruption of that period. By "that period" I mean Indira Ghandi's, basically the '70s. Yes, I saw this as a terrible thing.

Poetry is very much about personal mythology, I think; it always has been. And poets do see things in archetypal terms. I think *everyone* really experiences things in archetypal terms. So whether it's the Maharani, or this guy Sadaam . . . If he's not an ogre out of a fairy tale, what is? He really fits the bill. You think of that Goya painting of the Titans. Yet we're not considered realistic with such emotional responses to the world—by people who see things in quieter terms. For better or worse our work comes out of those feelings.

ELLIOTT: In your poem, "The Progress of the Soul," you say, "I've grown quite good at ignoring them, these street beggars. . . . "

RAY: Very ironic.

ELLIOTT: Ironic, yes, but I'm wondering about the degree of truth in it. Did you find yourself, when confronted with this sort of situation in India, actually having greater difficulty at dealing with such things than you might have anticipated?

RAY: Obviously you can't respond to everything. Henry James says, "Try to be one of those on whom nothing is lost," but if you were you couldn't survive a day, right? So certainly you cannot just be torn apart by suffering. But I don't think I would ever want to be like the people I was characterizing in that poem. The irony sometimes in my poems is very, very heavy to me, and yet I will come across someone who has misread that and says, "This guy is really terrible. He says you should ignore beggars." So actually there were a couple of poems I wound up putting quotation marks around. You know, this was "the ugly American" take. In fact, maybe I was a little too hard on the ugly American. I mean sometimes, after all, the American *is* doing his best.

ELLIOTT: I think it's difficult to read that poem, despite being aware of the irony, and not recognize just what you are saying—that there's a degree to which just to survive you must pull back.

RAY: Yes, in a new poem (not new—it's one that just bubbled up recently, but it's been walking around with me for a long time) I talked about what I had in mind when I went to India, because I knew it would be a big problem to confront this, and I said to myself, "Well, I will just pretend that we're not there. I mean, after all, our destiny was to be some place else, so I will just pretend that it's a total fluke, a kind of dreamy happenstance that we are there, and therefore I will simply not respond. And I found that just didn't work, and we were really torn apart by a lot of things. I'm reviewing a novel right now about India in the early 70's, and it brings back that life—mosquitoes everywhere, smells, sewage problems, sick children all around, diarrhea, crowds of people. America was very strange after India because you look out a window and there aren't people out there. There aren't people in the fields, there aren't people on the grass, there aren't people milling about everywhere. So you come back here and everything looks very strangely shorn and barren and depopulated. And then four years ago we spent some time in New Zealand, which is as opposite to India as you can get, because it's still a very unspoiled country. They're working on that real hard. I mean they are working on catching up, but it's a country where you can drive for forty-five minutes cross-country and not encounter a single car on a main highway.

India is still very much in my mind. One of our daughters married an Indian boy, and some of those people we got to know in India are still very close to us, and some of them have since come to this country. India is very much in our blood to stay. It will be very strange to go out to New Zealand and Australia again. There's a sense of unreality about those places that are still not afflicted with population problems.

ELLIOTT: Recently I saw a reference to Plato's feeling that ignorance is the cause of evil, so that idea is there in one of the cornerstones of Western civilization, but it is not one that seems to have taken root as an idea as firmly as it did in Buddhism. In some of your Indian poems, and in particular "The Razor's Edge," the concluding poem in *The Maharani's New Wall*, you allude to Buddha.

RAY: The Noble Truths, for instance.

ELLIOTT: Do you find the Buddhist view of the world compatible? Is it one that has attraction for you, as seems to be the case in the last poem?

RAY: Oh, very much. I'm not a good Buddhist by any means. I'm a Quaker, but I'm not a good Quaker either, and they very much are in agreement about all kinds of things—certainly non-violence. To me it seems perfectly manifest, for example, that people shouldn't have guns. There's a lot of wisdom in Buddhism, and I find myself very much calmed when I read anything about Indian philosophy or Buddhism. I mean, there are many truths, and mostly we don't relate to them. But even a little bit helps. This whole thing about living in the present—not to be sucked into the past, grieving for the past, fearing the future—the need for centering and staying in the present . . . It's very important. Doesn't America need that desperately?

If there's one thing wrong with our kids, perhaps it's that they don't know how to sit still for an hour. This constant feeling that if things aren't revved up every minute they'll fall apart—that's the kind of anxiety that destroys them. As you know, my son was destroyed by that. If they could just learn to sit still. Kids need it so desperately.

ELLIOTT: The Buddhist sense of compassion seems quite evident in *The Maharani's New Wall* as well as in your earlier poems.

RAY: Life basically is a mystery that we don't understand and never will, and that's why I feel so intolerant of somebody like Bush thinking he has the ability to understand so much about these situations he can fix with hardware. It's also a dilemma for writing. Remember that when someone asked one of the Buddhist masters if he wrote, he said, "Well, of course not." That struggle for peace of mind is a very different thing than struggling to write. So if I *really* wanted to be happy, I think I would quit writing. It's a very painful trade-off sometimes to realize that those very things that I know keep me unhappy—the monkey mind and struggling with all these painful issues—if I just wanted to be happy or enlightened, if you will, I would drop them. It is a struggle between silence and words. So when I opt for writing, I know it is choosing in pain. The dog goes back to its vomit. I'm choosing struggle and pain and the world of no answers when I could give myself some serenity.

You see this in meditation, and in Quaker meditation certainly, when you leave off meditating, because something that's come to you seems so very important to get hold of. *That's* writing, the disease of clinging to ideas.

ELLIOTT: Yes, but one of the things that I find appealing about both Quakerism and Buddhism, as opposed to some aspects of Hinduism, is the commitment to confront the world and not just withdraw completely into some meditative state.

RAY: Yes. When the Iraq bombing started, this particular conflict hit me very hard because I had been feeling some peace in my life, and I knew that if I expressed my feelings there would be friction with my neighbors and so on. I thought, well, this is a challenge to hide my feelings, to pretend I don't care. And I couldn't do that. And of course we talked about it in [Quaker] Meeting, and it wasn't a matter of whether we could really succeed in doing anything about it either; it's just that I came around to feel that, yes, we have to express what we feel and think here, and I belong with these people. For better or for worse I don't belong with those people who are waving their flags. And if they come and put tables on top of us and jump on them, then that's where we belong; but we can't be lifting tables and turning them over and putting them on top of other people and jumping on them simply because they are not the people we belong with. It's a very cruel world, and this business of deciding where we belong has been a big thing with me. And I've also found out that I don't belong among the fashionable poets. I'm not a *New Yorker* poet and never be. And yet I've longed as much as anyone to be glamorous. That's a big thing in our life, after all—to be glamorous, to get an Oscar or to be Miss America. These are big things for us—to be in that fashion gallery. But we must finally accept that's not what we are. We are something else. Altogether.

Note

Ray, David. *The Maharani's New Wall and Other Poems.* Middletown, CT: Wesleyan University Press, 1989.

V. The Surprise of Writing

A Conversation with Robert Morgan

Ithaca, New York
January 1992

Robert Morgan (b. 1944), born in North Carolina, has written nearly as many books of fiction as of poetry. *The Strange Attractor: New and Selected Poems* was published in 2004. He has taught at Cornell University since 1971.

ELLIOTT: The first thing I want to ask you about is your most recent book, *Green River: New and Selected Poems*, which is now just a few months old. How did you approach the task of going through all your former volumes and making selections? What sort of principles did you use in putting together this volume?

MORGAN: I found it difficult to select down to only eighty-some pages. The publisher told me the book had to be 93 pages or less, so I had to go back through seven books and select the text that was less than 93 pages. The first thing I did was go through my notebooks and try to figure out the chronology of poems, partly just out of curiosity to find out when the poems were originally written or the first draft was written. I did a lot of that kind of background work to get some sense of which poems followed which. I have several friends who have read my poems over the year, like Michael McFee and William Matthews, and I asked them for suggestions of poems they thought should be included.

But beyond that, I took what I thought were the best poems and my favorite poems and put them all together to see how many pages I had, and then I took out some until I got some 87 pages. I wanted kind of a sampler of my work, something that would represent the whole range of it. For that reason I left out several poems that I would have included, because they seemed like others that were already chosen. I wanted a book that would give the reader an idea of what I have done, the kinds of poems I've written, from the very short poems at the beginning, the experiments in narrative and rhyme forms in the 70's, the science poems of the early 80's, right up to the present.

ELLIOTT: I remember your saying at the reading in Scranton last October something about how you were surprised at the number of poems you chose that, when you looked at the manuscripts, were virtual first draft/last draft poems.

MORGAN: That really surprised me because I had been telling students for years about how much revision it takes to write poetry. I had the impression that I have worked over my best poems many times, but I discovered that roughly ninety percent of the poems that I wanted to include had only minor revisions after that. Of course there's the other ten percent that were very heavily rewritten often over a period of five to fifteen years. But apparently there really is such a thing as inspiration. When the juice is flowing you go with it. [Laughing.]

ELLIOTT: "First thought, best thought." Isn't that what Allen Ginsberg says?

MORGAN: It took me by surprise. I felt as though I might have been not practicing my preaching.

ELLIOTT: Has it changed either your preaching or your practice since you discovered this?

MORGAN: I'm a little more careful in telling students that I work through many drafts of my poems. In fact, I have mentioned this to classes. Another thing I discovered looking at the notebooks was that the poems are usually written in clusters. I sort of knew this before, but I hadn't thought about it much. I realized that over the past 25 years I have had periods when I would write very little. I was always writing something but not very much, through several weeks, a month. Then I would start writing again and usually do two or three poems that didn't quite work out, before I got to one of the better poems, and then I would write three or four or sometimes more, then go through another dry spell. It seemed to be cyclic, but I couldn't find any principle to it. It wasn't seasonal. It didn't seem to have anything to do with whether I was teaching or not. So I have no idea what the real chemistry behind this is. Maybe that's better. The surprise of writing and the sense of discovery and unpredictability are probably important to a poet. You don't know when you can do your best writing, so you keep trying and you stay hopeful.

ELLIOTT: The title of this book and many of the poems in it mention place names which are from the Carolinas. It seems as if most of the poems have that geographical location. Without reading the little blurb on the back of the book, people would hardly know that you've lived in upstate New York for twenty years. How do you feel about that? Is there some hesitancy to deal with the area that you're now living in? I know that there are some poems that could conceivably be set in upstate New York, but when they specify an area it rarely seems to be here. I think there's one poem where I saw the word "upstate" and thought that must be a New York poem.

MORGAN: Well, it surprises *me* to some extent. I feel as though the Blue Ridge Mountains of North Carolina, the Southern Highlands, were just given to me, almost, as a subject and a location. I was born there and grew up there. It seems that very little writing has been done about that area.

94

It's fresh and unused by American writers, and it's an opportunity. It just happened that I grew up there and knew it. I had no plan to write about the Southern mountains, about my family. When I was young I thought of myself as a poet who could write about anything. When I thought of other poets I thought of Baudelaire in Paris and Pasternak in Moscow. I didn't even think of myself as a Southern poet. But as I continued writing poetry and trying out subjects and voices, I discovered that I had this material which I could use and which was really exciting. It was something that had been given to me which other poets didn't have. Very few other poets had written about that area at that time. I can remember the excitement of realizing that I could write poems about hog killings or farming—just the most ordinary things. [Laughing.] I remember being asked by my father at one point back in the late Sixties, "Do you think you can make poems out of just anything?" That was part of the fun—to realize that, yes, you could write about almost anything, things that ordinarily are thought of as not worth looking at twice, but that they often are the *best* subject for a poem.

I also got more interested in the mountains after I left them and came to upstate New York. It was as though I could see them more clearly, and I began to write poems about my family and stories that had been told to me by my grandfather, sort of folk stories. I began to read about the history of the Southern mountains once I got to Cornell, to really study it. But I have written about other things, poems about science and technology and gadgets, and even a few poems about upstate New York, which is also part of Appalachia. But in both fiction and poetry I feel as though I have been given material which I couldn't resist writing about.

ELLIOTT: A similar phenomenon, it seems to me, is that when you write poems about family, again they are memories of your family in North Carolina. Your family here in Ithaca doesn't seem to appear in your poetry very much. Would you give the same sort of answer to that, or do you feel, as some people do, that family poems about one's own wife and children have been overdone?

MORGAN: I think that poems based on memory are often much more successful than poems based on recent experiences. Whoever said the muses are the daughters of memory knew what they were talking about. One of the functions of poetry is to remember and to make alive things in the past. I don't know if this is true of other writers or not, but for

95

me one of the most crucial things in writing poems or stories is finding the right subject matter. If you get the right subject, the right character, the right incident, the right metaphor, you're inspired to write, you really want to follow through; and I have, for better or worse, followed the ideas that seem to come to me. I wanted to write about some things that maybe not a whole lot of people knew anything about. I've tried to look at people from inside as opposed to outside, to somehow get behind the stereotypes of Southern highlanders, poor people. To tell events in the 19th century from the point of view of people who have not had much of a voice in fiction and poetry. I find that really exciting—to be able to get into the mind and to find the voice of the character, and let them tell the story, to really tell it from their point of view.

ELLIOTT: At this point in your career, what percentage of your time and energy do you put into writing fiction as opposed to poetry?

MORGAN: I began as a fiction writer in my teens and really edged into poetry in my early twenties, got increasingly interested in poetry and started learning about poetry. I wrote less and less fiction in the late Sixties and eventually abandoned fiction about 1970. For a decade, I concentrated on poetry and critical prose. I did a lot of essays back then. But in the early 80's I got interested in fiction again and started writing it alternately with poetry. One of the things I discovered, to my pleasure, in the mid-80's was that I could work on both—just go back and forth. I didn't stand on any ceremony. I'd write a poem and go back and write a story. In recent years, late 80's, I have been writing more fiction and less poetry. I still write both and I want to continue to write both. I feel they are cut from the same cloth, with similar subjects. Short stories are in fact very similar to poems, especially free verse poems. I guess I'm increasingly interested in lives in both poetry and fiction.

ELLIOTT: Has the increased attention to fiction changed your poetry in any significant way?

MORGAN: Not that I've noticed. If I have an idea about a character that needs to be treated in detail, I obviously go to fiction and not poetry, because poetry is so much more compressed as a medium. It depends on implication. It's a very implicit medium. Prose can include the details, can go more deeply into something. For a while, writing fiction made me more interested in formal poetry. Writing narrative prose made me feel the appeal of forms in poetry more.

ELLIOTT: You have talked elsewhere about the rather significant changes that began to occur in your poetry after *Red Owl*. Having put this book together, in which you can see different phases and styles in your poetic career, do you feel that your poetry is on the verge of any other major change of that sort, or do you feel pretty comfortable with the ways that you've been writing in recent years?

MORGAN: No, I'd like to try some new things. I don't know exactly what they're going to be. That's the fun of it. One of the things I want to do is go back to working on a long poem I started on in the early 70's and never finished. It's a very long poem. I think I have more than a hundred pages of it. There are many things I want to try in poetry and I haven't.

ELLIOTT: The few new poems in the section at the beginning of this book seem almost like a cross section because there is quite a range of different styles there. So as I was looking at them I was wondering if you felt there was any one certain direction that you were tending to go in more than the others—perhaps the greater philosophical density of something like "Middle Sea." Or, because of the sonnet in that section, I wondered if you were going in an even more formalistic direction.

MORGAN: There may be a direction I'm edging in, but part of the excitement of writing is you never know quite what you're going to do until you do it. I don't have any sense of picking out this direction or that. I would like to continue to experiment with all kinds of poems. I'm very interested in formal issues in poetry and trying new forms and perhaps even different voices and styles. But as I said before, I think the thing that really triggers poems for me is subject matter. If I have a subject that excites me enough I will start working on it and usually stay with it until I get the poem written. I'm more a content-oriented poet than a form-oriented one. I really am interested in stories, landscapes, nature, science, that sort of thing—particularly metaphoric connections between different levels of experience. Often poems start with a metaphoric idea, some very unexpected connection.

ELLIOTT: I'm interested in the relationship between the great number of nature poems and what you call the science poems, to which I would add what I think of as technology poems. I know that you started out in math and moved away from that into writing. What is the appeal in terms of subject matter of science and technology, and how to do those poems relate to what you have been saying about the appeal of memory, family, geographical location, and so on?

MORGAN: I've always been interested in objects and the poetics of objects. I can't explain it, but I love to write about the perception of things. Somebody has compared my poetry to German *Dingegedichte*, which means "things poetry." It's a tradition in German poetry. I've always loved imaginative perception of the world and objects, and I've felt that they are important—to rediscover things that seem very ordinary, to see them in new ways. We're surrounded by machines all the time in the modern world. It seems that we have a kinship with them. One of the things that poetry can do is find out about those kinships and express them in seemingly new ways. One reviewer said my poetry was very democratic; it was willing to consider not only other people but things and stones and trees. I never thought there was any real split between people, landscapes, and process in nature. I love the tradition of poetry that somebody like Whitman belongs to, who is willing to say, "I'm the poet of the body, I'm the poet of the soul." The spirit and the physical world seem to be the same thing; they are located in each other, and poetry reminds us of that connection. It's one of the things the poetic imagination keeps rediscovering.

ELLIOTT: Whitman is certainly the American poet of getting it all in.

MORGAN: You find very few truly gnostic poets. There are a few, but most poets perceive this world as image of other worlds and are not just trying to escape it. Poe would be an exception. But poets like Dickinson, Emerson, Whitman are very much interested in experience of this world, at least as analogy or metaphor of experience of the spirit.

ELLIOTT: Two of the more recent poems in *Green River*, "Vietnam War Memorial" and "We Are the Dream of Jefferson," with its line about the "painful dissonance of the present," both border on being political, which your poetry does not usually do directly. How do you feel about political poetry, and are those poems about as close as you would want to go to what many people think of as political poetry?

Morgan: I would prefer the word "historical." I'm very interested in history, and politics is certainly part of history. One of the things I want to write about more in poetry than I have is history. I believe American poets have ignored history for some reason. The way we understand who we are is to know something about the past—political, cultural, spiritual, artistic. But in recent years I have tried to write more about the study, the experience of history and incorporate the historical sense and vision in poetry. I've done it implicitly from the very beginning, but that's harder to see. I've always been very interested in the presence, the haunt of the Indians, who were here before us, and the way in which political history and cultural history inform the present. I've treated history more explicitly and in greater depth in fiction than in poetry. It seems those poems you mentioned, "Vietnam War Memorial" and the Jefferson poem, deal much more directly with the reality of history, and it *is* political.

But for some reasons not clear to me, American poets have always had a lot of trouble dealing directly with political issues. In a sense there's no need for poets who deal directly with current issues because so few people read poetry. [Laughing.] If you want to have an impact, a political impact, you need to give speeches and walk a picket line and write editorials to reach people. But I don't think poets should forget political implication, and I think it's good that occasionally poets, like myself, who write about nature and things that seem apolitical are challenged by the political. That doesn't bother me, but I'm much more interested in the historical sense and seeing things in the perspective of long periods of time, and the political is certainly a part of that. A poet like Wendell Berry, who is very much involved in ecological and agricultural issues, certainly has his greatest impact as an essayist and lecturer and not as a poet, though his poems and prose are very much related.

Elliott: I was just going to mention him. Do you feel a kinship with the types of things that he does, as another Southern writer working in both poetry and prose?

Morgan: I certainly do. I admire Wendell Berry. I probably have a less positive sense of the small family farm than he does because I grew up on one that was very poor and went through the struggle with my parents when I was a child and saw how difficult it was to survive. I understand he came back to the farm as a grown-up and has had a very different experience with it. No, I feel very close to his vision of American agriculture and to a poet like Gary Snyder's vision of the wilderness and the feel of the wilderness. Those two are very different things, though people tend to equate them. Primary interest in agriculture is very different from an interest in wilderness.

ELLIOTT: Snyder is another poet who has an interest in gadgets and tools.

MORGAN: In the technique and the way things are done. I share that. It's one of the ways to enjoy the world, to do things well and to really care about the craft of making things, doing anything, whether it's farming or cutting logs or repairing tools. If we lose touch with that, then we certainly have lost an important part of culture.

ELLIOTT: A word that comes to mind when I read much of your poetry is "definition," both in terms of details—something having definition, having much sensual detail—and also in the sense of defining something. In many of those thin poems of yours, like "Rear View Mirror" or "Odometer" and also in a poem like "Cedar," you are in a sense creating definitions by listing associations and metaphorical implications. As I was reading some of those poems, I was reminded of one of my favorite poems from hundreds of years ago—Herbert's "Prayer," a sonnet defining prayer. Do you feel much kinship with the Metaphysical Poets in any way?

MORGAN: Well, I like them, but I don't know if I feel a special kinship with them. I do with some of the Romantic poets, and epigrammatists like Robert Herrick I feel very close to. But I believe that definition, as well as redefinition, is one of the things that poetry does. When I was a very young poet, I had the idea that every poet creates his or her own dictionary. To some extent they redefine words and find for them the truer definition. Poetry invents and renews language, and as Emerson says, "All words are fossil poetry." Language comes from poetry and not the other way around. It's the poetic delight in naming and renaming for which language exists, and a poet is rediscovering, to some extent reinventing, language, finding the true name or true definition of something. This is always present in poetry, poetry of all ages. If you are satisfied with the current definition, you wouldn't write poems, perhaps. But I've been told that I write poems that are not unlike Anglo-Saxon riddle poems, gnomic poems that describe or define almost as a teasing game.

ELLIOTT: The last words of Herbert's poem are "something understood," which is a marvelous way of ending it. The kinds of definition poems you write seem to be striving for that.

MORGAN: The awesome thing about Herbert to me is the simplicity of his poems—the cleanness on the surface and the depth *in* the poem. They are poems that seem so direct and yet you can't exhaust them. There's a lot of wisdom and experience in them. I prefer a poem that has a spare, even austere, surface, with most of the richness inside it.

ELLIOTT: You mentioned the Romantic poets. Which are the ones, of the British Romantics, you feel the most affinity for?

MORGAN: Certainly Keats, and Wordsworth. Some of Coleridge's poems. But I was thinking more of the American Romantics—Emerson, Whitman, and Dickinson (if she's a Romantic). I think of all of those as coming out of the Romantic movement, of American poetry of the 19th century as really being inspired by the British Romantics and particularly by Wordsworth and Coleridge. It's as though the two strands of American poetry come right out of the two sides of Coleridge's brain: the Wordsworthian affirmative side, and the symbolist, gnostic side. [Laughing.] When I first started reading poetry, the poems that interested me were things like Pound's translations of Chinese. They seemed like the most wonderful things I'd ever seen—the simplicity, the poise of those poems and the depth and subtlety underneath that very quiet surface. The first poet that ever really attracted me, I believe, was Whitman. I remember reading Whitman in my sister's college textbook she had brought home from Bob Jones University, and I was taken that somebody could make gestures like Whitman did in "Song of Myself." I'd never seen something like that. I remember thinking, "Wow!"

ELLIOTT: I wish I had been introduced to "Song of Myself' at an earlier age, but my first introduction to Whitman in high school was "O Captain! My Captain!" and some other shorter poems that I don't particularly care for. It wasn't until I got to college that I was really introduced to "Song of Myself."

MORGAN: I was introduced to poetry in a way that was much better than I understood at the time. We had to memorize poems in the sixth, seventh, eighth and ninth grades and get up and recite them, and I really learned some poems then that I carry with me ever since, things like Bryant's "Thanatopsis," "O Captain! My Captain!," Sydney Lanier's "Marshes of Glynn," Poe's "Annabelle Lee," "The Raven," "Daffodils," by Wordsworth. I went to a school that was so poor and so old-fashioned that it concentrated on things like diagramming sentences and memorizing poetry.

ELLIOTT: You mentioned Pound's *Cathay*, and in *The Generation of 2000* you mentioned that you have written a few haiku early on in your career. Could you say more about your interest in Oriental poetry?

MORGAN: My first teacher was Guy Owen, the novelist and editor, and he had us write haiku. He introduced us to Oriental poetry in translation, and come to think of it, that's where I first encountered *Cathay*, in his class. A wonderful teacher. But it wasn't haiku that impressed me most; I think it was the slightly longer poems, more Chinese poems than Japanese poems by people like Li Po and Tu Fu and an earlier poet, T'ao Yuan-ming, from the Fifth Century who is sometimes called the Chinese Robert Frost.

ELLIOTT: What relationship do you feel to what has been called in recent years the Neo-Formalist movement? There is an anthology edited by Robert Richman, with people in it like Brad Leithauser and Dana Gioia, which tries to make a case for formal poetry as being the way of the future. Similar sorts of pronouncements elsewhere elicited articles from Ira Sadoff and Marvin Bell in *The American Poetry Review* talking about their feelings concerning what they perceive as the limitations of the Neo-Formalists. How do you feel about that movement?

MORGAN: I think it's inevitable that poets rediscover traditional form after a long period of experiment in open form and free verse. The forms and devices of traditional poetry are so powerful and provide such muscle to poetry in this language that it would be inconceivable that poets wouldn't go back to them at some point and use them. So that makes sense to me. What you discover, of course, when you experiment with poems, is that form itself is not enough. You still have to have the idea, the content, the voice, the passion, the obsession when using forms that you have with any other poetry. But I don't think the key to good poetry is in having form or not; it's in other things. It's really in the human spirit. It's in having passions about ideas or peoples or things. But some of my favorite poetry in the 20th century is the formalist poetry of Yvor Winters, who I think is a model for the New Formalism, both in his theories of poetry and in his own work. He is a very great poet and most of his poetry written after he's about 28, I think, is in very traditional forms—almost entirely iambic trimeter or tetrameter. I think young poets would do well to go back to poets like Winters for a model, or to Robert Frost who's always a formal poet. But Frost is not a great poet because he is a formalist; he's a great poet because he has a great vision of the world, a great understanding.

I believe that probably in the next few decades poets will go increasingly back to traditional forms that have been so useful in English over the last 1000 years. There's a reason they discovered those forms and used them; they work. They carry a lot of force. On the other hand, it's deadly in American poetry if you sound too much like a British poet or sound too literary. This is why I mention Winters. Winters understood that poetry in rhyme and meter had to talk naturally and plainly, and it had to have content. The trick is to do both at once, to have a voice, to speak naturally, to speak dramatically, to tell a story in the poem and not be dominated by the form. It takes years of practice to learn that. The poet who has learned it can, like Phillip Larkin, say "form is nothing, content is everything," because he's such a master of form that you don't notice it when you read his poems. But I believe it's natural to English to write on a four-stress line, something like common meter, and for most poetry it's natural for it to rhyme. Rhyme is a device that really works in English. For more elevated poetry you don't need either. That's why Whitman works so well. He's writing in a very elevated voice, often using incantatory techniques, using the psalms as models, the gospels and Ecclesiastes. But yes, I'm very interested, if not so much in the poets you mentioned, in the idea about going back to form.

ELLIOTT: In the workshop in Scranton I believe you said, "Arbitrary lines will be the way of the future."

MORGAN: Arbitrary lines, arbitrary forms. You have given up an important dimension of poetry if you don't have an arbitrary form through which the natural voice of poem can play. As you write in sentences and rely on cadence for rhythm, you approach prose. The power of poetry is often in the way in which the cadence, the natural flow of language, is played against a form that is arbitrary, say a sonnet, a tetrameter line. Frost called that the breaking of the English sentence over the end of an iambic line. It's just one of the powerful effects of poetry. You can have it both ways in traditional forms. You can have the arbitrary unit of the tetrameter line, or the pentameter line, plus the natural music and cadence of the sentences. Free verse poetry loses that, the ground base, as it were, of a meter. Rhyme is somewhat different. Rhyme gives you yet another escapement mechanism, to use John Frederick Nims' term—counting off time. The poetry is in measures of several kinds. It has the measure of the natural cadence; it has the measure of line, the visual line, as opposed to the sound unit of the line; it can have the measure of rhyme and the measure of the stanza, with all these simultaneously going on. And that creates quite a polyphony, as it were. A lot of modernistic art is impoverished because it gives up so much of the resources of the media. In abstract painting you've given up the power of representation, not to mention narrative or allegory. In free verse poetry you gain something, but you also lose quite a bit too.

ELLIOTT: Free verse has been dominant for quite a while now and probably is still dominant in most writing workshop programs, judging from the work that seems to be coming out of them. But some people say that if you want to write free verse, you really should know how to write more traditional metrical verse. Can that formula be reversed? Is there anything that mastering free verse gives you in writing more formal verse that you would not have if you had not tried to master free verse?

MORGAN: Somebody who has learned to write very good free verse has already learned about the compression of language, which is essential to poetry; about the freshness of diction, which is essential to poetry; about the variation of cadence, which is essential to poetry; and they probably have an advantage in that they could bring all of that to their work in formal poetry. On the other hand, we are creatures of habit and if for twenty years we've been writing one way, it's sometimes hard to stop and go back and write in another. The danger is that if people are concentrating solely on the traditional forms, they may lose the sense of those three factors, which are essential to poetry. You've got to have it all. Part of the beauty of poetry is that it draws on all the faculties—memory, imagination, the sense of surprise, drama, narrative—all at the same time. It can't be just one of these things. If you have the compression and naturalness of free verse, plus this other game of form, you obviously have a richer medium.

ELLIOTT: To my ear it rarely seems that your poetry is as close to iambic as somebody like Frost, at least not as the norm. For example, in some of the new poems at the beginning of *Green River*, including those that have rhyme schemes, there may be an average of eight syllables per line—in a sense a tetrameter line—but they don't sound as iambic as Frost.

MORGAN: If they are iambic, they are what Frost calls loose iambic. [Laughing.]

ELLIOTT: When you are writing poems like "Middle Sea" or "High Wallow," how consciously do you work in relationship to the iambic line?

MORGAN: Not very much at all, for many of those you mentioned. My interest in the 80's was in combining forms, in writing, say, what was essentially a free verse or at best a syllabic line, and combining that with rhyme, so that it sounded as free as free verse in some ways, but it would have a pattern of rhyme. On the other hand, sometimes I wrote very metrical poems that were unrhymed and often had different line lengths. I got interested in ways of combining different kinds of poetry in new combinations and not going all the way toward doing everything traditional at once. I believe that kind of thing actually works pretty well for modern American poets. It's one way of trying new things, and keeping some of the old.

ELLIOTT: That's what seems to me to make your more formal poetry more interesting than much of what goes under the name of Neo-Formalism.

MORGAN: It's deadly if a poem sounds like a literary experiment. No matter what form it is in, it has to sound like it's spoken by somebody who really has something to say, concentrating on the emotions, the perceptions, the subject matter, and not just an exercise. If it sounds like form is dominating you, and the whole purpose of the poem is to write that form, then we have lost much of what we go to poetry for, which is experience. The music of poetry comes from the idea, the content, as much as it does from the actual stressed and unstressed syllables. You can write wooden language that is in iambic pentameter. That's verse as opposed to poetry. If you've lost the content and the passion and the vision, and gained a form, then in a sense you've lost everything.

ELLIOTT: In some of those poems I was mentioning it seems as if the ghost of tetrameter is hovering over it, but you may have three, four, five, even six stresses, at least to my way of hearing it. What sort of affinity do you feel for a prosodist like Hopkins and his sprung rhythm?

MORGAN: I feel great affinity for the *poet* Hopkins, if not for the prosodist. [Laughing.] I think the affinity I feel for Hopkins, besides just his vision of the natural world and his sense of awe and the presence of God in nature, is the way in which he rediscovered the heavy Anglo-Saxon line. The fact that he calls it sprung rhythm is in many ways irrelevant. What he discovered was a heavy alliterative sound that is always in great English poetry from the time of *Beowulf* to Robinson Jeffers and Whitman. A lot of times critics, prosodists, seem to be looking in the wrong direction, for something different in Hopkins. They're looking for sprung rhythm because he described his poetry that way. In Jeffers they're looking for a Greek line, because his father taught him in Greek when he was young. And in Whitman they're looking for something else. But in fact, if you know Anglo-Saxon poetry, you can see these great poets keep rediscovering this heavy broken line that has been in English from the very beginning—the heavy accent, alliteration.

I love his poetry but I get lost in his prosodic theory. I admire his prose, particularly his letters and his journals. I really love the vision and passion and voice of his poems. In fact, one of the delights is to keep discovering sonnets that you passed over earlier. He has a very small collected works. But some of the poems are very difficult to get into. I'm still discovering Hopkins. He's one of those poets like Dickinson that you just can't exhaust. You think you know Hopkins but you read another one of his poems that you had completely forgotten or never really read before, and Wow! You see what he's getting at.

ELLIOTT: When I was thinking about the relationship of some of your poetry to the iambic line, the title of your book *Sigodlin*, came to mind. I'm wondering if in a sense what you are saying about people who are mere versifiers is that their poetry is anti-sigodlin and that a dose of sigodlinism is healthy for poetry.

MORGAN: I love the word "sigodlin" because of the sound and because it seems so strange, even though I discovered that the source isn't so strange. It was apparently a contraction of "side goggling." [Laughing.]

But yes, there is a crookedness and a slantness to experience, and being too geometrical and too perfect goes against that. It's crookedness of experience often that is most significant. But what's the quote that Emerson likes, "God writes straight in crooked lines"? [Laughing.] But it is also interesting how you can contrast the crystalline lattice of verse's perfection to the roughness and skewedness of experience. Some of the important tension of poetry is between these two things, and it is not unlike the tension in poetry between the narrative voice and the lyric stasis of the poem, the stasis usually coming from the metaphoric depth—that sort of timeless experience with the connection in the metaphor—and that being in tension, in some sort of balance with the *saying*, the motion of the poem, the narrative of the poem. It is important to have both. Every poem talks, has a voice. But almost all lyric poems have that spark of metaphoric connection, which is not motion.

ELLIOTT: Given the shift in your poetry toward being more formal, what do you think of as the greatest achievements in free verse in American poetry, or do you not return to many of the freer poets with pleasure anymore?

MORGAN: Well, the greatest achievement in free verse is certainly Whitman. He is the great monument in American poetry, along with Dickinson and Emerson.

ELLIOTT: I was thinking more of the 20th Century.

MORGAN: There are very few masterpieces in the 20th Century in free verse. I believe the poems we go back to are poems that are variations of traditional forms: Stevens's great blank verse, the blank verse of Eliot—the play between traditional forms, like sestinas, and blank verse in the *Quartets*. Jeffers might be my model of a great free verse poet. Roethke stretches out into some free verse toward the end of his career, echoing Eliot in the *Quartets*, echoing Whitman. But the great revelation of American free verse is still Walt Whitman, I think, and the way in which he broke out of the traditional line through the discovery of Italian music and the free-flowing line of bel canto opera, and how he felt free to use all these rhetorical gestures he had heard in the Bible. But poetry is not only in verse; some of the great American poetry is in prose: the prose of Emerson, the prose of Thoreau, the prose of Faulkner, the prose of

James Agee. There are many ways to write poetry, and verse is only one of them. But I guess I would pick Jeffers and possibly D.H. Lawrence as great examples of free verse poetry, though I believe that what Jeffers was doing at his very best was recovering, as I said, the old Anglo-Saxon line, sprung rhythm, if you will. [Laughing.]

ELLIOTT: Did the Pound/Williams strain of American poetry ever appeal to you?

MORGAN: Not Williams very much. Williams appeals to me as a man and as a critic, and I feel I should admire him, but none of his poems ever reached me the way some other poets have. Pound very early appealed to me as a theorist of literature and language. But both of those always seem to be relatively minor poets compared to T.S. Eliot and Stevens. I probably like Williams's short stories better than his poems, and the single text of William Carlos Williams that I admire most is his essay on Poe in *In the American Grain*. I have read essays by Williams that are so good that they made me proud to have tried to be a writer.

ELLIOTT: You wrote once, "My understanding of tradition is that our language and our age are writing us in ways we can't always see." A number of people over the years have commented on the impoverishment of the language, the effect of mass media and television in particular. Do you feel at all pessimistic about the future of language or poetry? Are there ways in which the language of our age may have a negative effect on poetry of the future?

MORGAN: I grew up without television for the most part, and I've always felt a little bit out of sync with my contemporaries for that reason. It's impossible, or course, to know what the effects of the electronic media are quite yet. But I believe that writing seems to be going better in the parts of the country that were only more recently affected by television. Some of the most exciting writing is coming from the South, from rural Maine, or from Montana—the outlands. [Laughing.] It could be that those places still have a closer relationship to story telling and an oral tradition. But it is clear that we have had probably more excitement in fiction writing in the past twenty years than in poetry. These things seem to come and go. In the 50's and 60's the excitement was with poetry. I believe to some extent that the revival of poetry in this country was inspired by Dylan Thomas's reading tours. He got people interested in poetry and poets. The most exciting writers of the past two decades have been fiction writers. I'm not sure why that's so. Poetry and fiction seem to trade places somehow in American culture. In the 19th Century after the explosion of poetry writing—Whitman and people like that—the best writers in the late 19th Century were people like Twain and James who wrote great fiction. Why this happens I really don't know.

ELLIOTT: Do you feel, from the point of view of somebody in a university literature department, that the great interest in critical theory over the last twenty years has had a positive effect in terms of the readership for new poetry and prose?

MORGAN: The world of literary theory seems not to have affected creative writing in one way or another, but it has affected the critical community; and indirectly I think that has affected writing, because all the attention given to literary theory has taken attention away from fiction and poetry, so what the poets especially lack is a critical audience. Poets are there, the poets read poetry and they sometimes even write critical articles; but what's missing are the critics we used to have who serve as interpreters and intermediaries with the audience. The academic critical community affects the journalistic critical community a great deal. What American poets lack now is not only academic critics who might have turned attention to them, but *The New York Times* and *The New York Review of Books* and that kind of critical notice that is essential if you want to reach a bigger audience. There's a wonderful audience out there for poetry if you can reach it. On the rare occasions when I'm invited to read to a public library or at a community center, I find it. There are some good listeners to poetry, people who like poetry. But for the most part you may have no way of reaching them except through poetry readings.

 I don't think academic critics have ever been the ones who made readers read poetry or fiction. But I think that reviewers in big magazines and newspapers do. When *The Los Angeles Times* and *The New York Times* quit reviewing poetry and talking about it, that hurt the audience of poetry a great deal. But it is connected with the academic critical community because, to some extent, those critics take their signals from academic critical writing.

 On the other hand, poets are lucky perhaps that they don't need large audiences. Poetry is the only literary art that seems to thrive with just a few readers. [Laughing.] In fact, I believe that the most necessary audience for a poet is to have one or two very good readers. We spend our lives looking for those one or two true readers, the readers who really understand not only what we're doing but what we might do.

ELLIOTT: What was Whitman's comment about "great audiences"?

MORGAN: Whitman was very optimistic. [Laughing.]

Note

Morgan, Robert. *Green River: New and Selected Poems*. Hanover, NH: Wesleyan University Press, 1991.

VI. Home Keeps Getting Bigger

A Conversation with Naomi Shihab Nye

La Plume, Pennsylvania
March 1992

Naomi Shihab Nye (b. 1952) has received awards for her poetry, fiction, and children's literature, including the Robert Creeley Award. Her books of poetry include *Red Suitcase* and *Tender Spot: Selected Poems*. She teaches creative writing at Texas State University.

ELLIOTT: Storytelling and narrative are very important in your poetry. Where did appreciation for a good story come from? Who were the storytellers in your family?

NYE: We grew up inside our father's rich fabric of Palestinian folk tales. Since we didn't live in the Middle East when I was a child and he wanted us to have a sense of the landscape, characters, and dynamics of village life, he told us traditional folk stories but also invented his own. He's a wonderful storyteller, and my mother is also a master of detail and description. She was a painter and helped give us a sense of visual wealth—in museums together—some of my earliest, happiest memories. I remember her teaching us how nothing is flat. So very early I had a sense of how one could grow up inside a tapestry of voices and words. When I was small in St. Louis, Carl Sandburg was still alive in Chicago; some of my first and only TV memories were of watching Carl Sandburg on public television saying his poems. I just loved that sense of getting lost in a story, of being swept away—how much that could add to one's life! And now, older, I feel continuously reminded of how surrounded we are by poems and stories, in every cafe, neighborhood, and airport we pass through. The excitement of paying attention feels sharper and more delicious even than before.

ELLIOTT: So was this just a natural tendency that worked into your poetry, or was it more of a conscious, artistic decision?

NYE: No, I think it was more an inclination. I recall talking with students at Saint Bonaventure University in Olean [New York] and they were saying, "Your poems tend to be like stories. Do you like only poems which are like stories?" I don't. I also love poems which are dense, word forests, lush and lyrical, richly imagistic. Sometimes the term "anecdotal" is used to indict a poem, and I often feel like defending it. Why *not* anecdotal? What else is this life? We *need* the anecdotal, too, or at least a method of perceiving and honoring anecdote as part of the whole. I think I've worked to find some kind of natural-sounding voice that can tell a tale in a poem, whether a big or slim one, but hopefully lyrical, mysterious elements may enter in as well. That "sacred blur" that people talk about?

ELLIOTT: Do you have a sense of that type of poetry being somehow necessary these days? It seems as if the storyteller tradition is one that our society has lost, and poetry like yours, to my mind, seems to fit into that gap.

NYE: It's an honor you would say that, especially having just heard Hayden Carruth today, who feeds that hunger so marvelously. I felt all caught up in the northern Vermont world just listening to his poems and the voices of his neighbors; and I think there's a kind of restlessness in our society for the feeling of attention which listening to a story gives. That's the gift of it—to be lifted out of the swirl of your own life and suddenly, by way of story, be taken completely somewhere else.

I recently returned from the Middle East where a student asked, "Is it true that in America everybody is so busy they never do what they really want to do?" Of course, my instinct is to negate a stereotype whenever I hear one, but I started thinking about people I knew and how many want to do things they're not doing right now. Isn't there a real restlessness, an urgency for something more amidst all the schedules? Maybe the sense of a simple story is one thing diminishing in contemporary culture. I think people need to sit on front porches again, and trade their days. Isn't that what people really hope for at holiday gatherings? The yearning that often isn't satisfied because there's so much going on. And I don't feel that television dramas fill that need.

ELLIOTT: There is a word that shows up in various forms in many of your poems that is obviously related to what we are talking about—"memory," "remembrance," "remembering," and so on. What do you feel is the role of memory in your poetry?

NYE: Well, *everything* is memory, yes? It's obvious: What happened ten minutes ago is memory already. It's the native ground out of which all of our stories come. I find it very important to remind students how much *invention* is a part of memory, that those of us who would like to change our memories, in effect, can. I think that's one of the gifts of art and have certainly seen people who are burdened or haunted by memory finding ways to change it. Writing is one way we *can* reinvent what is given to us, literally, to remember and make something *else* of it, something *other*. That's the power we need to carry on.

I remember being three years old and feeling nostalgic, and wondering clearly, "What am I missing?" It was a strange sense of homesickness for something much greater than I could analyze or name.

I was very interested in an essay that Gerald Stern had in *The American Poetry Review* in the early '80s about the importance of nostalgia as a certain sense of being-in-exile which is crucial to art, closely connected to the impulse to want to put words and images together. I have always felt there is more of a *need* to remember than we could ever identify or measure or explain. The older I get, the more excited I am about the pliable aspect of memory and what we can do with it besides just accumulate it.

ELLIOTT: Do you ever feel any tension between the impulse toward memory and giving attention to the present moment? Some poets' poems are very much present-moment poems.

NYE: No, I think they serve one another. What we take note of in the present moment is so related to what our memories have constructed in us, what we are able to see, the kind of perception that we have, it's hard to separate them. Sometimes memory begins intruding—we may want to tell or invent too many possible remembered things while trying to write something more present. That's one thing I'm grappling with in two new poems I'm working on right now—too many past images keep cluttering up the immediate body of the poem. To write them I've had to live through a small history of certain perceptions, yet I don't want to include *all* those perceptions in the poems; I want the pieces to be immediate to the scene that's presented. So I keep slashing things out and trying again. It's a constant balancing back and forth, as well as a forging into new ground.

ELLIOTT: Three of the important elements contained in your poetry seem to me to be narrative (which we just discussed), imagistic detail, and what I would call wisdom, sometimes presented parabolically and sometimes more straightforwardly, even as overt advice (as in "The Art of Disappearing" and "Kindness"). Do you ever feel a tension between the first two of those elements and the third? Many poets want to avoid sounding didactic. Is that a risk you are less or more willing to take in your recent work?

NYE: I'm trying to get over this innate instinct to give advice. Where does it come from? The by-product of general enthusiasm? Of course, I've really only been giving it to myself all this time. If anyone else can use it, take it. Maybe it's what happens to those of us who read *Aesop's Fables* when we were children. But I always thought the morals were unnecessary! The stories seemed more magnetic and mysterious without them. I'm working on it.

ELLIOTT: Is there any music that has been important to your sense of poetry? Is there any relationship between it and your poetry?

NYE: Perhaps *all* music I've experienced—either as listener, songwriter, or singer—has connected to a sense of poetry—the resonance, the rhythm, the relationships—each word as note. I grew up in a singing house. My mother had, still has, a beautiful voice which carried us into sleep each night. We were never shy about singing in front of others or opening our mouths in general!

As a teenager I realized many other people found lyrics of songs more immediate and easy to respond to than words written on a page. I was beginning to write songs in those days, and they felt like *cousins* to poems. I've always been intrigued that one has never, *never* become the other. That is, I've never started a song which later became a poem or vice versa. Obviously there's a distinction, but I know they feed one another, and we are lucky when poems come singing into our heads, slowly, slowly, one line, one phrase at a time. We learn to listen, perhaps, the same careful way we listen to music we love.

ELLIOTT: In *Yellow Glove* there seem to be several poems in which the connections are more oblique, more freely associative than in much of your earlier work—poems that don't tell a single story but present a collection of observations. I am thinking of ones like "The Tunnel of Questions," "The Spacious Air," and "Grateful." Is this a direction you see your poetry going in?

NYE: Yes, I feel myself more attracted to the web of interconnected images and implications, the nonliteral, unexpected journey in and out of a single story which causes a poem to feel less narrative in a consecutive or chronological way, but more thickly layered—rather riskier and odder, sometimes, too. Writing as a continual experiment—if we let it be—keeps traveling out into new territories, examining them, circling home. And home keeps getting bigger.

ELLIOTT: You mentioned your background of Palestinian folk tales, but what else has your bicultural heritage contributed to your poetry?

NYE: It's contributed so much to my life that it has to have something to do with my poetry. It's given me a sense of being at home in many places, feeling at ease—very little has ever seemed *strange*.

      Since my father was an immigrant in his twenties, and retains to this day a very strong link to his first land of Palestine, I grew up quite conscious of *elsewhere*. My father embodied a sense of longing for elsewhere, even as he lived here, and the sense of worlds connecting. Perhaps that's enlarged my whole horizon of *listening*. The Middle Eastern culture is a deep and involving one in many ways, and I feel lucky to participate in parts of it which are meaningful to me—family, heritage, connection with story and land, and long, long history. Once I studied German for two years so I might feel a similar connection with my mother's heritage, but it didn't take. I forgot everything I learned. She's always stressed that she's an *American*, anyway. Recently a box of hundred-year-old letters has made those Germans come alive for me for the first time. I think biculturalism gave me a keener sense of detail, and a tip of the head that's rather wry.

ELLIOTT: You have written a lot of travel poems. I suppose that can be another source of multicultural awareness, but what is the appeal of travel to you? It almost sounds like a stupid question, because it's hard for me to imagine anybody not being interested in travel, but . . .

NYE: Well, a lot of people *aren't* interested in it. One reviewer in Texas wrote of my poems, "Why doesn't she just stay at home and eat Spam like the rest of us?" I can't believe that's what the rest of us are doing. I don't think anyone *needs* to travel to have something to write about, but my life has tended to be a traveling, nomadic life, from growing up in Saint Louis, moving to Jerusalem when I was a teenager, moving to Texas where my family had no real ties, and traveling widely in and out of Texas ever since. Texas itself is a richly interesting crossroads place. Many say it's easier to pay attention to detail and experience when you're in a place that's not your own, and I recognize the sweet allure of poems which come from being somewhere so briefly that everything feels fascinating. It's not exotica which interests me. I rarely write things immediately when I'm in a spot. I don't sit here today and start a poem about Pennsylvania.

I may write notes and impressions, but I usually wouldn't try to make a poem or story that included them until a long time later, until the details had filtered into a larger web of consciousness. So I don't think of travel as a gimmick or a trigger; it's just been my life.

ELLIOTT: In "You Know Who You Are" you ask, "Why do your poems comfort me?" Was that poem written for either William Stafford or W.S. Merwin, whom you have mentioned to me as two writers who have touched your life significantly?

NYE: "You Know Who You Are" was written specifically for the poems of David Ignatow, although some people have thought it was for one of the two hero-Williams: Stafford and Merwin. Of course it *could* have been for one of them. It's for anyone whose voice startles or soothes us into clarity. The small change of words becoming articulate and precious again. Words bearing real, simple weight again.

ELLIOTT: Is that the way you hope your poetry gives comfort?

NYE: I would hope that, now and then, my poems might give readers a renewed or sharpened sense of their own lives.

ELLIOTT: In your comments about Merwin in *The Amicus Journal*, you refer to his "very profound hope . . . for wider perception" with regard to environmental concerns. You sound as if you share that hope. Where does it come from?

NYE: Pessimism seems intrinsically useless. When we weigh all the information we have—impending and present environmental breakdown, critical overpopulation, poverty, grim cycles of violence in too many places of the world, even at the end of the twentieth century (it astounds me)— it's easy to feel disheartened. But if that's *all* we feel, what motivation or energy exists to move things along toward more hopeful possibilities? I'm convinced that energy—the encouragement of positive energy in our lives, in whatever minor venues we may operate in—stimulates hope. If we don't have that, we have nothing.

ELLIOTT: You haven't published many overtly political poems, but one is relatively recent—"Trouble with the Stars and Stripes" in *Mint*. Is this an area you would like to move into more often?

NYE: A real sense of human empathy is the most political thing I know. And empathy being a gift of real communication, poetry has power or possibility to bring distant lives into focus. In terms of poetics, this means everything: dissolving the sense of *other*. When Palestinian students have told me they can't write the details of their own lives because their writing must focus on their cause, I respond, "If you *don't* write about your own lives, no one will really know you. Headlines won't do it. Rhetoric won't do it. Our cause *needs* the substance of personal details." If we really knew one another, we couldn't be enemies.

I think even vegetables are political.

ELLIOTT: Empathy seems to be powerful for you then—a possibility for connection with people, or vegetables—a kind of politics, as you say. Some poets feel that the connection between their poetry and ordinary people's real lives is rather tenuous, or they don't much care, or they think of poetry only as an aesthetic experience and make distinctions of that sort that I'm not terribly comfortable with. It seems to me from your poetry that you probably aren't comfortable with those divisions either. But is that assessment accurate? Aside from the purely literary or aesthetic, what do you envision or hope for in terms of the relationship between your poetry and readers' real lives?

NYE: I hope that relationship is close, and immediate. Yes, I'm a champion of poems which allow us to see or feel our lives differently, so naturally the poems which interest me most are those that spring out of some daily, tangible ground. Obviously different kinds of poems do this for different people. And no, debates about aesthetics have never been my forte.

ELLIOTT: I was thinking of a poem of yours, "What Brings Us Out," which is not overtly a poem about poetry, but it would seem to me that's what you are trying to do with your poetry—bring people out.

NYE: Hmmm . . . Well, you're the only one who has ever said that, but perhaps it's right. Yes. The person in that poem who spoke for the first time after three years was in a poetry therapy class in San Antonio. Preparing for our group each week, I realized I felt much more interested in how poetry could be a vehicle for healing than I'd ever felt in "aesthetics of poetry" or "poetry as art." And together we witnessed the power of an image in a woman's poem which enabled the man to emerge from his three-year silence. It was a tame image for her, but a triggering revelation for him, releasing his history, as he realized the image held *no pain* for her. Somehow that allowed him, for the first time, to step out of his own pain and take control of it in a new way. *This doesn't have to hurt anymore.* By the way, he taught the class when I left.

ELLIOTT: How wonderful.

NYE: It *was* wonderful. A confirmation that poems can help us, that poems continually bring us into new understanding of our own experience, whether they're our own or someone else's. And, yes, thank you for saying that about the poem. That's one of those gifts, of course, that we can't ever plan.

ELLIOTT: Another thing I was wondering about, and if this is too personal a question and you don't want to deal with it . . .

NYE: No, nothing is too personal.

ELLIOTT: About your poem, "The Little Brother Poem". . . did your little brother read it, and what was the effect? Again, the question is one of the relationship between poetry and real life. Did that poem play a role in any sort of transformation?

NYE: A very strong role. I'd never been more nervous about a person recognizing himself or herself in a poem and made sure I sent it to my brother before it was published. His reaction startled me. He had a friend engrave it in metal so he could hang it up in his office! When we talked about it, something healing and positive happened—I consider it a positive transition in our relationship. Acknowledgement can be such a liberation! It's been surprising, David, how many people have said that the line in that poem, "I'll take differences over things that match," has caused them to make a phone call. Teachers and students have said, "Well, I hadn't talked to—my sister—my friend—in twelve years, but when I read that poem, I called her."

ELLIOTT: Isn't there another poem, about somebody's death, perhaps, where you talk about making a phone call, or where you could have and you didn't?

NYE: Oh, that's "El Paso Sky," a little piece in *Mint*. Actually it's not me in that poem. But it's that sense of regret that is present to some degree in all our lives. I'm constantly trying to learn how to live better with regret, how to be better friends with regret, or let it motivate me usefully rather than just wallowing, which is so terrible. Actually that piece may connect to the man who hadn't spoken in three years. Once when I went to El Paso, I met a woman who told me she had scarcely been out of her house in two years since her husband's death. Driving around town, she commented about the sky of El Paso, which is one of the great skies of the world. She had forgotten how the sky looked from different angles and at different times of day since she'd been in her house so long. Gee, if she had come out sooner, maybe she would have started feeling better sooner. We ended up talking about regret—actually she had very particular regrets about her husband's life as well as death. And she had a clear, careful voice, which I tried to write that piece in. I guess it could make you make a phone call too. [Laughing.] I've made a few, just rereading it.

Probably we all need to write about family at one time or another, a vulnerable area, of course, but maybe one that matters most. And there's that wonderful magic that happens which extends *family* consciousness—if I read about your grandmother, I'm given my own somehow again. So yes, the little brother.

Notes

Nye, Naomi Shihab. *Different Ways to Pray*. Portland OR: Breitenbush Publications, 1980.
_____. *Mint*. Brockport, NY: State Street PRess, 1991.
_____. *Red Suitcase*. Brockport, NY: BOA Editions, 1994.
_____. *Words Under the Words: Selected Poems*. Portland, OR: Eighth Mountain Press, 1994.
_____. *Yellow Glove*. Portland, OR: Breitenbush Books, 1986.

VII. Precarious Balances

A Conversation with Stephen Dunn

La Plume, Pennsylvania
March 1993

Stephen Dunn (b. 1939) won the Pulitzer Prize in 2001 for *Different Hours*, one of nineteen books of poetry published since 1974, including *What Goes On: Selected and New Poems 1995-2009*. He taught for many years at Stockton University.

ELLIOTT: You have talked elsewhere about the incorporation of abstraction into your poetry. I don't want to cover tenitory that you've already covered, but I do have a couple of follow-up questions. Even though you have left behind some of the teaching you received in the writing program at Syracuse with regard to imagistic concision and so on, would you have had it otherwise? Do you feel that being subjected to that discipline, and subjecting yourself to it in your early work, made you better able to incorporate the sort of abstraction you like in your poetry?

DUNN: I think that my experience in graduate school couldn't have been more valuable for me. I didn't know anything. I was a history major as an undergraduate, and I had been away from school for seven years. I was an English minor and I had read the great poets of the tradition, but I hadn't really studied or thought much about contemporary poetry. I think not only the discipline in graduate school was important, if it were that—I'm not sure I would even call it that—but what was very important was that everybody had high standards: Philip Booth, George P. Elliott, Donald Justice, W.D. Snodgrass. I learned more from the high-mindedness of those people than from any specific thing or lesson they offered. Probably what I took away from that experience was a sense of holding myself to rigorous standards, whatever they might be. Those writers were all good enough that they didn't seem to mind very much if students went their own way. The concision and imagism, which was not just tacitly advocated in the writing program at Syracuse but was probably part of the poetic culture at that point, was something that I'm very happy to have been exposed to. It's not very useful to depart from places where there is no solidity. Whatever departures I've made from that kind of training are from a solid place, I feel, a place I'm happy to have in my past. My teachers all were formalists, each in his own way. When they wrote free verse, it had the rigor of their formal measures behind it. Each was in the process of accommodating his style to new possibilities. I was very lucky to be exposed to them and their work.

ELLIOTT: I want to talk about a particular aspect of craft: the music of poetry. I read your interview with Philip Booth, a poet whose sense of rhythm seems to be connected to individual stresses, playing off of a ghost iambic, and so on. Yours does not.

DUNN: Right. That's true. It's hard for me to say anything about this except that I do know when I'm in what is my rhythm, and it usually has something to do with repetition and recurrence. Certainly that's true in "Loves," where I work the rhetoric of "I love . . . ," "I love . . . . " The dilemma in orchestrating that poem was to build so many repetitions of a similar rhetorical nature and yet to vary them enough so they wouldn't be monotonous. I don't know how to talk about it. I think the music in my poems, beyond the use of repetition and recurrence, has more to do with tonal shifts and emphases more than any regular stress pattern. And when I'm working well—this is true of most poets—my language is always seeking, and I hope finding, companionable language. Sonorous friends.

ELLIOTT: Of the different types of music found in poetry, it is the syntactical—the cadences of syntax—that is often the most evident in your work. You seem to me to be very much a poet of sentences. Not all poets are, of course. But when I'm reading or listening to your poetry, it is the variety of the sentences that provides much of the rhythmic interest. When you write a sentence, it starts a trajectory, and when the sentence comes to an end, the voice lets us hear that, very definitely, but along the way I never know whether there are going to be a few more dips and turns before you get to that point, or how long it is going to be. I think of that as being musical.

DUNN: That's interesting. Yes, I think so. Also, I think of myself as working often in a kind of dialectical way in a poem, in a kind of statement and counterstatement manner. If my poems have tension, it is largely because they are either doubting or refining the claim that has just been made. So it is that kind of movement of the mind (and I hope a little bit of the body too) off of what has just been said that is connected, I suspect, in some way to the sound of the poem, the music of the poem. And yes, this is reflected in the pacing of sentences, and the rate at which they disclose information.

ELLIOTT: Charles Wright has catalogued the different types of free verse in American poetry, the different lines and senses of line breaks in Whitman, Williams, Eliot, early Stevens, and so on. Which of those traditions, or others that I haven't mentioned, have you felt yourself a part of?

DUNN: Well, it's interesting, because I'm teaching this semester a Frost, Williams, and Stevens seminar, and the poet I find myself most kindred to of those three and maybe in general is Frost, though of course I don't compose (except in the way I've learned from him how to tell a story in a poem, or perhaps from his sense of narrative tact) in the way that he does, and I don't have iambic underpinnings. When I move to Williams—whom I once felt much more kindred to in terms of diction and movement in a poem—I find that his line seems increasingly foreign to me, except in the later poems. I feel a great closeness to, say, how he moves in "Asphodel." I know I must have been strongly influenced by that, not so much the triadic stanza or the so-called variable foot, but how to speak directly and to orchestrate such directness. One of the essays that I've been reading of Williams is called "Against the Weather." I think by temperament, more so than I, he was adversarial, and his wish was to go against whatever the prevailing weather was, and that's often how he got the juice and tension in his poems. I admire that. But when he decided finally to relax his line and really to negate his own dictum, "No ideas but in things," that's the Williams that I can hear and follow so much better. But I love the way Frost tells stories in his poems, and I love that Frost is almost always if not overtly, implicitly philosophical in his poems, which I wish to be also.

ELLIOTT: There are lots of poets for whom line breaks are very noticeable in one way or another. Your line breaks seem to me not to call attention to themselves. How do you feel about that?

DUNN: Oh, I think about them a lot. Line breaks are very important to me, especially, when I've been working with that three-line stanza of mine with the tucked-in line. Though when I read those poems, I read through my line breaks. But in terms of arranging the poem on the page and of orchestrating the poem on the page, it's very important to me where I break the line.

ELLIOTT: I don't mean to imply that it's not. Perhaps what I'm saying is that it's the art that conceals art.

DUNN: Yes. When I found that three-line stanza (and I think of Williams' definition of a line as a unit of attention), it became an extremely important way for me to edit my own poems, of finding out what a line would bear, just how much it could tolerate until it must snap into the next one. I did pay rather strict attention to this when I was working with that stanza, and I still do, but more and more I've been working in kind of block form with a line that's somewhat longer. Almost all of the new poems in the *New and Selected*, the fifteen I've chosen, are in block form. There are maybe two that are not. My three-line stanza made me, for years, judicious about lineation. Now I want to let my line accommodate more variety, more emotional and intellectual range. Or so my recent poems seem to be instructing me.

ELLIOTT: What I mean by line breaks that call attention to themselves would range from Robert Creeley or Denise Levertov, on the one hand, who work out of the Williams tradition, to someone like Sharon Olds, who for other reasons ends many lines with words like "of" and "the." What she says is that she doesn't want the reader to linger at the end of a line at all; she intends those endings to just whip you back to the beginning of the next line.

DUNN: No, I *do* want to find a way to put pressure on my line, even when I'm working discursively, apparently discursively. And mostly I recognize the value of breaking a line on a stressed syllable, to propel it into the next. To break on unstressed syllables often causes a slackness, though one can think of many exceptions.

ELLIOTT: Do you recall an essay by Greg Orr, called "Four Temperaments and the Forms of Poetry" (*The American Poetry Review*, September/ October 1988: 33-36), in which he speaks of the relation between four qualities of poetry in terms of which ones are the strongest for particular poets? I was wondering where you place yourself in terms of the two sides of his quadrant: story and structure, on the one side; music and imagination on the other. One of the things he says is that if a poet's strengths are all on one side or the other, there are problems. He thinks of somebody like Dylan Thomas as often being weak in story and structure, and relatively too strong in music and imagination. He says Shakespeare is right there in the center, strong in all four temperaments, but most poets tend to have a dominant one or two.

DUNN: I have a couple of thoughts about that. I think Thomas at his best does have a good marriage of sound and sense. I love those poems— "Fern Hill," especially. But I do think that poets of a strong lyrical bent often disappoint because they are insufficiently interested in the story inherent in their poems. A lot of poems I see wish to tell stories—they flirt with narrative, they suggest a narrative—and then won't give in to that impulse. They'll become distracted by lyrical effusion, or something. I suspect that, when I fail, I give in too much to content and may forget that content needs the vivacity of language and rhythm to make it palatable. But I would like to think that in my story poems and in my most personal poems, the imagination is very much a player and that the poems are essentially fictions, which have their own music. I'm never satisfied with a poem that hasn't taken on a fictive life, or that hasn't found a language that compels me to respond to it as much as the content issues in the poem do. So I think any good poem, a poem that really holds up, probably has sufficient qualities of all those four categories.

ELLIOTT: As I reread your work, I was noticing the points of view you use: poems where you say "I," poems where you say "he," poems where you say "you," "we," or "they." I went through the books and charted out how much you used each one. In *Full of Lust and Good Usage*, for example, you have a lot of "you" poems, ones which address a non-specific "you." Then they tended to disappear. There were none whatsoever in *Not Dancing*. As for the number of poems in which the protagonist is a "he" or "the man" (but more likely "he") they were most evident in *A Circus of Needs* and the last three books. Given those four or five choices, why have you tended to choose one or the other at different times in your career? Are there ways in which using "he" allows you to deal with certain subject matter that you would not be able to deal with if you were using "I"?

DUNN: Yes. I've mostly chosen to compose in the first person, but I try to worry about the dangers inherent in it: self-congratulation or pity, solipsism in general. The "he" is often somewhat of a distancing device. I often tend to write my poems in first drafts with "he," to achieve a distance from self, and change it to an "I" in a later draft. It's a frequent compositional habit these days for me—maybe in the last six, seven, or eight years—to begin a poem "He did this, he did that," and get a lot of stuff out and then convert it to "I." I'm sure it's just a way of tricking myself into invention and to give myself latitudes and liberties.

ELLIOTT: After largely disappearing for a while, there are more "you" poems in *Landscape at the End of the Century*, but three of them aren't a generalized "you." "You" is Bartleby, for example, or "you" is innocence—a very specific "you." Do you feel the generalized "you" strategy became a stylistic tic for too many poets?

DUNN: It *is* a problematical device, because often the "you" is indefinite. It is often a closet "I." You wish the person did say "I." It's fraught with difficulties. I think that's all the more reason, though, in my present thinking, to try to write "you" poems. Because of the difficulty of getting away with it, it seems eminently worth trying.

ELLIOTT: In putting together the *Selected Poems*, did you learn anything interesting? Were you surprised? What was the experience like?

DUNN: I guess if I was surprised, it was that I liked so many. It's terrible. I thought I wouldn't. Therefore it's going to be a large *Selected*, close to 300 pages including the new poems, which by the standards of selected poems these days is somewhat indecorous. [Laughing.]

ELLIOTT: Did you leave any out?

DUNN: You have to realize that I was selecting from eight books, all of them rather sizeable books, and I did manage to be severe with myself in the early books, I think. But increasingly, from *Not Dancing* onward, I found myself fond of a lot of the poems; and I had, for good or for ill, a great fondness for a lot of poems in *Work and Love* because that was my book that did the least well. It was a book that was important to me when I wrote it; it covered poetic territory that mattered to me, and still does. And so I think I've chosen liberally from it. That was the surprise—that so many of them held up for me. It might be just some fundamental error of character on my part that I can't get rid of more poems, but I couldn't, and that's the major surprise.

I found myself eliminating poems that many people had liked chiefly because of their subject matter, so that a poem like "Weatherman" was omitted because it feels compositionally sloppy to me. It feels like I put almost no pressure whatsoever on the lines, that I was content with merely being interesting. And I was drawn to, say, smaller poems that don't have as much richness in content as that one has, but which were, to my present way of thinking, much better made. I got rid of several poems like the one the woman at lunch today said she liked, "Poem for People Who Are Understandably Too Busy to Read Poetry." It just seemed to sprawl, and it seemed overly jokey.

ELLIOTT: Both of those poems played well, when you used to read them.

DUNN: Yes, they did. People loved to hear them. But they bothered me on the page.

ELLIOTT: In your eight books you have about 350 poems, which is a large number. Do you ever feel there is any danger in being able to write so many poems? Are there any drawbacks for you? Or is it never enough, and there's no negative side?

DUNN: No, no negative side whatsoever.

ELLIOTT: It's nothing you have to work against?

DUNN: It's an interesting question. Maybe we're always apprentices—even now. But I know that the first ten years of my writing life was apprentice work, and what apprentices should do is write a lot and try out new things all the time. And so back then I never stopped myself when I was, say, mid-poem and the poem was only going to turn out to be a tour de force. Now I do. I work very slowly now. I don't work slowly when I *start* working, but I don't start working very much. I wrote very regularly; I had great writing habits for about fifteen years. I think the sense of how difficult it is to write a truly good poem has slowed me down. I no longer wish to write a poem that is just pleasing and works. I want something of consequence or I won't continue it. The writing that I was doing back then I don't mind thinking of as a kind of practice. But actually it never seemed to me that I was working a lot. I had a two-or three-year head start on the second book, so that when the first book was finally accepted (this happens to most poets, I think), I had almost enough poems for the second, but I withheld it for a while, so that the first one got published in '74 and the second in '76. It seems like fast work, but in fact the '76 book was five years of work—four or five years of composition. I've always spent three or four years of work on a book. It's not terribly fast, and I've just been lucky enough to be rather fertile. I consider it all a good thing in the sense that poems prepare you to write other poems. But for whatever reasons, I'm working more seldom. I work when I feel something of some dimension coming on—all the things I tell my students not to wait for. Except when I go to the writers' colonies, where I work every day. I still like to do that, and I'm capable of doing that only there. I work five hours a day at Yaddo or MacDowell.

ELLIOTT: How often do you go?

DUNN: I go once a year for two or three weeks, and I work every day. I never have an unproductive day at those places, and in the last several years I tend to work on poetry during the morning and prose in the afternoon. I always end up with fourteen or fifteen poems, some of which are close to being finished. But I don't even worry about that. They are really poems to work on for the whole year, to shape and refine and extend. Look, it's all important and it's all vanity at the same time. So few of our poems will survive, if any.

ELLIOTT: Well, let's go forward 100 years to when the poets of today who are remembered will be remembered by only, say, four or five poems. Do you have any sense of which those might be? Among all of those 300 pages in your *Selected*, are there some that really stand out for you, about which you would say, "Yes, this is what I would stake my career on"?

DUNN: It's really hard to say. I think the "Loves" poem remains the most ambitious poem I've written and is a kind of culmination of a lot of previous poems on similar subjects that I've done over the years. Maybe that. There are several poems in *Between Angels* which seem of some significance. "Tenderness" is one of them. But I mean these are my choices. Somebody who was doing a marriage anthology just told me that my poem "Epithalamion" in *Landscape* was the only poem in the language written for a second marriage, which pleased me. I thought it was so when I did it. There are poems that can last for the oddest of reasons, at least for a while. Right now it matters to me that my *Selected Poems* represent me as I was, as I am. Which ones will last is really for others to say.

ELLIOTT: Do you ever find yourself surprised at what an anthologist might choose?

DUNN: Yes, always surprised. The Norton person who chose the four poems for the anthologies I'm in chose perhaps a few that were *au courant*. They dealt with sexual politics; they dealt with matters of skepticism in regard to faith in the individual. I would have chosen others. But I have no complaints—I'm fond of all four of those poems.

ELLIOTT: When you were talking about choosing poems for the *Selected*, it

132

was interesting that you said the ones from *Not Dancing* onward seemed to be the strongest, because when I reread your books, that one seemed like a point of demarcation for me as well. It was the last four books that seemed to have fully reached a certain sense of maturity. Before that, it was more scattered.

DUNN: I actually believe that the mature work begins with *Work and Love*, the book right before. From that '81 book on, I would say I found something like my own way of moving and thinking in a poem. Maybe my own voice. Early on, in the first two or three books, I wasn't working against very much. I was essentially learning what I could do. I think Donald Justice's poems influenced me enormously. I still love them, and loved the care in them. But for a long while I would always think whether he would like a poem of mine, and I stopped doing that somewhere around *Work and Love*. While still admiring Justice, I did not want to write like that. I found it, in fact, constricting. I needed to talk much more in poems, and I found a way to allow myself to talk.

ELLIOTT: In your interview with Philip Booth, he said that he thinks you can be most effectively influenced by poets who are not like you. Has that been your experience?

DUNN: I don't know. I remember him saying that, and I've become very interested in it. Reading Ashbery, say, who is a poet I think is brilliant but whose poems don't matter to me, I'm interested in the way his mind behaves in a poem and the associative movements he makes in poems— all things that are quite removed from the way I usually work. I think in the new poems that I've been writing, I've allowed them to be much more associative in thought, much less sequential and logical. And it's very possible I've learned from someone who is not my kind of poet. I think it's quite possible. I mean, one can admire the quality of mind and the skillfulness in Ashbery and still want poems with a greater emotional base than he will allow himself.

ELLIOTT: Influence questions are always problematic, but after rereading your Cheever elegy I'd like to ask how much he was an influence on your poetry.

DUNN: A good deal, I think. You know Frost's great line in one of his essays that if it is with outer seriousness it must be with inner humor, and if it is with outer humor it must be with inner seriousness. I think Cheever exemplifies that in his stories. When the stories are most pathetic, I find myself laughing my ass off. They're just beautiful, and my laughter is often the laughter of recognition. At his best, he's a brilliant manager of subject matter. In his stories which are broadly comic, there's this wonderful pathos underlying them. I love those two tones. Whenever I can blend tones of that kind in my work, I'm very happy, the humor, say, servicing some deep concern, some sense of gravity beneath the surface. Or the gravity leavened by some word-play. Yes, the storytellers. I've been writing some essays and remembering some stuff about people that were important to me. Do you remember Jean Shepherd? I was such a private, quiet child and teenager, even though I was an athlete and seemingly had more of a life than I did. I was so quiet and didn't speak to anybody. I used to listen to Jean Shepherd every single night at ten o'clock on my radio in my room, and he articulated my whole childhood for me. What those stories did was make me feel less strange than I was, because I thought only I was thinking things like that. And he was so funny, of course. I grew up on those stories, and when I think of telling stories, certainly in my regular life, just oral stories, there is a lot of Shepherd that I hope I've refined and made my own. And I think Cheever is important, and so is a lot of Dostoevsky and Melville. They first made me aware of the power of literature. It was the great philosophical novelists that excited me the most.

ELLIOTT: This next topic may be one that you've been asked about a lot and has been overworked. I'm thinking of basketball. There are certain words that you tend to like, like "pivot" and "corners" and "edges"—spacial metaphors that seemed to me possibly to be coming from someone for whom corners and lines and pivoting and so on were important in terms of movement of the body in a game. Has basketball entered into your poetry in that indirect way?

DUNN: I don't know. In my "Basketball and Poetry" essay, the way I found myself talking about it was not in any of these specifics but in the broader sense of transcendence. Basketball was my first way of having a chance to be better than myself. And poetry offers the same possibility, that you can exceed yourself, you can be better than yourself, though there are greater undersides in poetry, of course. By exceeding yourself, you may find out things that are not particularly sanguine, that are troublesome. I think that's why one yearns for the purity of basketball, in which there is transcendence without terrible consequence. That's the adolescent dream—to perpetuate play forever. Whereas the moments when I've been better than myself in poems were often troublesome, because if you exceed yourself in a poem, often you may have learned something that was probably happily buried within your subconscious and went down there for a certain reason. [Laughing.] The words "pivot" and "corners" I think more likely come out of my shy past than my athletic past because it always seemed that I was turning away to avoid something, to get out, usually not having to speak, or being shy around girls and pivoting and hiding out. The "Corners" poem is about finding a corner in the middle of a room, some little *querencia* that will give you the illusion that you're safe there.

ELLIOTT: Turning to your most recent book, *Landscape at the End of the Century*, . . . your vision of the century's end is one that you sometimes express in terms of the absurd and references to Kafka. In a 1984 interview you portrayed *Not Dancing* as being melancholy and even negative compared to the books that preceded and followed it, and similarly there seems to be more of the dark in *Landscape* than in *Between Angels*. Then there is the poem "Loves" at the end of *Landscape*, which, of course, provides some balance. It's a very dialectical book, but the first two sections seem rather darker than *Between Angels*.

DUNN: Yes, I think they are, although every time I think I'm being dark, it always seems to be less dark than what a real dark poet would be offering. I mean my dark doesn't quite hold up as dark; there are too many scattered pleasures in it.

ELLIOTT: What is your sense of the end of the century? What meaning does that phrase have for you?

DUNN: It's pretty hard not to feel pessimistic about the century. I mean, with all the great discoveries and technological breakthroughs, not only are people not better than they were throughout history, they are almost collectively worse. One of the things that most disturbs me, because I feel complicitous in it, is how inured we have become and continue to be to atrocity. Hannah Arendt was absolutely right—the banality of evil. I remember when a girl got raped in my neighborhood when I was growing up. It was shocking; we didn't know what to do about it. We live with such facts and worse on the daily news every night. I guess in order to live in the world at all, you have to become inured. It troubles me enormously that it's very hard to muster outrage when something happens to someone you don't know. That's a terrible end-of-the century situation, and it doesn't seem likely to get better. Even though I don't write with any deliberate political consciousness, it seems inevitable that all of this would be in the poems one way or another, that the stuff of the world would enter and impinge upon them. Yet I do believe in local happiness; I do believe we can be wonderful to each other in the small. I hold out for such things. But in large, we're awful, we're an awful race. We're just dreadful.

ELLIOTT: Your poetry has gone back and forth between problems and pleasures, but it seemed to me that maybe that balance was getting more precarious. The organization of *Landscape*, with those two rather dark sections followed up by "Loves," enables you to keep the balance, but it is almost as if you have to write a poem as big as "Loves" to maintain it.

DUNN: "Loves" is just one of those gifts that comes along. I accepted it. But I do think you're right about the precariousness of the balance. Yet I don't wish to write any particular kind of poem or have any particular kind of balance. I just want to be true to that which presents itself to me.

ELLIOTT: "Loves " is one of those poems that seems to address a specific "you," rather than a generalized "you."

DUNN: It really isn't a person, though I can see how it could be read that way. As I was writing it, I thought I was addressing the poem itself and especially the fiction of the poem. I was addressing the poem. So when I talk about it being "my spacious one," and at the end, "my truest love," I know because of what just proceeded it that it resonates into the possibility that I'm talking about my wife too, and I don't mind that. But in fact, I'm addressing the poem as a fiction, which is my true love and that which has resisted me and given me possibility.

ELLIOTT: There are a number of poems in *Landscape* that seem to be "ars poetica" poems in a certain sense. Is that a subject that's been more on your mind?

DUNN: Yes, mostly having to do with the notion of the fictive. And I have in fact, in the new of the *New and Selected*, a poem called "Ars Poetica," which is a poem about composition, but it's a poem about restraint and how restraint is worthless unless you have something large to restrain. Restraint is an artistic principle which is uninteresting, I think, unless it implies holding a lot in, something that wants to spill over. But, to answer your question, yes, the more one has written, I suppose, the more one is inclined to find the act of writing, that which one has engaged in for many years, to be part of his (or her) subject matter.

ELLIOTT: Using the title of your book as a metaphor for a minute, what's your sense of the *poetic* landscape at the end of the century? When you look at our country's poetry now vis-à-vis twenty-five years ago, there seems to be such a greater variety.

DUNN: I think it's wonderfully rich. There may not be (though there very well may be too) those dominant figures that rule the landscape, but there's certainly a great deal of variety and much more intense pockets of interest throughout the country. The audience has gotten a little bit larger. It's certainly a tiny audience compared to, say, the audience that goes to the movies, but there is a great deal of interest and concern about poetry. I welcome the richness of our different writers, and inevitably with such variety you're going to have more crap than ever before, and we do have more conspicuous crap in the poetry landscape than probably ever was the case.

ELLIOTT: Do you have a sense that what is sometimes referred to as the postmodern attack on the lyrical ego, and the attacks by the Language poets (among others) on the representational quality of language, and the many related concerns of contemporary critical theory are on the increase or on the decrease, in terms of their influence on poets?

DUNN: It seems a little bit on the increase, but Language poetry does seem like essentially a peripheral movement, and I think it will be that until, if ever, there are some wonderful poems written out of those impulses and that kind of intelligence. There are some capable people working that way, but I think when you decide to compose poems out of essentially a theoretical complaint that you are first of all knowing much too much about what you are doing and therefore won't discover enough, and also that the poems will likely be cerebral. It's the same problem with the theorists themselves, the post-modern critics; it's so hard to find anybody of that stripe having a primary response to a text, like saying, "Wow, this knocked me out!" or "I love this," which is I think the only way for us to respond at first to work that matters to us. We get from them second or third responses, until it finally becomes an argument with themselves, and the text becomes just fodder. I find it thoroughly unattractive. They need to be astounded by the world and their lives, and they need not go about it programmatically. That's the death knell or any kind of art, when it becomes theory-laden. It was much more interesting when the Dadaists and surrealists were reacting as they were to the bourgeois culture of their time. It was radical, and somehow so-called Language poetry simply seems insufficiently radical.

ELLIOTT: You do a lot of readings. Philip Booth, on the other hand, said he doesn't do any. What are the down sides of giving readings for you? Do you understand his refusal to give readings?

DUNN: Yes. I think it's temperamental. I understand it as he talks about it, and I suppose I know the pitfalls. I mean the pitfalls are that you might write poems to be a showman, poems that only will work in the air of the room. You can write poems to get easy responses. You can do all those things. If you write your poems for the page, knowing that they will be also spoken, I think that's a safety net against writing for the broad audience, to please. At this point in my career, I like doing poetry readings. It's just that I don't like doing as many as I've been doing. I've been accepting almost every invitation because I need so much money to pay the tuition for the girls. I would like to do less and work more. But I like the contact that occurs in the best of occasions in a poetry reading, and there's occasionally a wonderful gestalt between audience and poet. People at my readings are often surprised that they understood the poems, which means, of course, that they come to poetry not expecting to understand.

ELLIOTT: The heritage of Modernism?

DUNN: Yes, and I don't wish to be messianic about it all, or think of myself as a person who's going to be a bridge, but we do need poetry that can matter to the willing, intelligent, non-specialist reader.

ELLIOTT: I'm of two minds about the attack on Modernism that occurs these days in some circles, I know that the Modernists have tended to scare people away from poetry, but I love so many of their poems that I certainly wouldn't join those who dismiss them, saying they turned poetry in the wrong direction.

DUNN: Well, what those poets did is teach us how to read them, so that the poems became accessible for us, I think. I mean, I find "The Wasteland" gorgeous, absolutely gorgeous in most of its parts. I find Stevens consistently wonderful, and I can be very happy reading him precognitively. Even when people like Stevens and Eliot were being difficult, they were offering the other pleasures of poetry—sounds and textures, just wonderful music. And the poems worked for us, finally, not unlike the way cubism did—we just had to see enough cubist paintings to know how to see them. They instructed us how. I think that's what the best of the High Moderns did. Difficulty, with surfaces that invite us to pay attention to it, is not a bad thing.

Notes

Dunn, Stephen. "Basketball and Poetry: The Two Richies." *Walking Light: Essays and Memoirs*, New York: Norton, 1993. 46-53.
_____. *New and Selected Poems: 1974-1994*. New York: Norton, 1994.

VIII. Finding a Distinctive Voice

A Conversation with Lucien Stryk

Scranton, Pennsylvania
April 1994

ELLIOTT: I would like to start with some questions about translating haiku. What elements of the original Japanese are you willing to sacrifice for the sake of producing a good translation in English? For example, with regard to the 17-syllable form, it is clear from looking at your haiku translations that you have decided not to try to bring that over into English.

STRYK: No. I have taken comfort, I must admit, in the many things said regarding the 17 syllables by people like Shiki. I think that, to be frank, Shiki was right, that there are moments when to try to force the poem into 17 syllables would be unthinkable, certainly in my eyes. I forget the number, but in my little imaginary discussion among haiku masters in the introduction to *Cage of Fireflies*, I have Basho speaking of the number of poems in a Shiki volume which have more or fewer than 17 syllables—an astonishing number! And then with Basho, of course, there is that famous instance of the crow poem with 18 syllables. Some of the schools, such as the Soun, would just abandon the 17-syllable structure on such grounds, saying that if Basho could do it, if Shiki invariably did, why should we be saddled with such a severe restriction? So, coming into this field as a translator of haiku, knowing that the Soun poets have no concern whatsoever about the abandonment of the 17-syllable structure, knowing that Shiki so often did, that on occasion Basho did, I have never felt any compunction.

Also, I want a free hand. My hope has always been to give a sense of the poem's vitality. I always sense it in the original, else I don't try to translate the poem. There are many haiku I would not try to translate because, though I am sure that for many good reasons they are more than acceptable to others, perhaps even very good to others, they are not to me. Not all haiku, even by masters, would in my judgment be on the par with many of the poems I've translated. I should say, in a way, *all* the poems, because I have felt about each poem that it was virtually a master work, and I include even the lightest poems by Issa. But, on the other hand, I have at times, I'll have to confess, been a bit impatient with some of the comments made by the antitraditionalists. I think that there is very good reason to follow the structure so long as one feels that one is not being forced by it into unfortunate decisions.

ELLIOTT: I was interested in your comment that Issa, in contrast with Shiki and Basho, was very traditional with regard to syllable count.

STRYK: Very much so. Issa idolized Basho, of course. We have to remember that Basho was almost always a traditionalist. There were the exceptions, but we must bear in mind that he wrote only about 1,000 haiku. He was extremely hard on himself. We get good evidence of this in the haibun. There is that piece I quote, as an epigraph, in *Cage of Fireflies*, where he says (I am paraphrasing, of course) poetry has been the great passion of my life. It has given me much pain. I have not always succeeded, but it is my life. And he speaks at the moment in his haibun of the kind of torment all serious poets must feel from time to time.

So I think that he would be seen as the great master because his struggle *was* with form, his struggle *was* with the necessity of getting things right. ShIki's struggle is not as great. When he said, as he did, somewhat ungenerously, that out of ten poems, Basho hit the mark only a few times, he was being honest, but very severe. I don't think many would agree with him. I don't. But he felt, as you know from my little imaginary dialogue, that Buson hit the mark more often—about seven out of ten, he gave him.

But the scholars (such as Makoto Ueda, who writes so learnedly on these masters) would feel that Shiki had every right to make the break with the past, and that in fact he resuscitated the art and brought it into the modern age, particularly with some of his ideas such as rensaku [a sequence of haiku], a wonderful idea for the structuring of sequences. For example, Fujiwara in our interview in *Encounters with Zen*, speaks of making sequences, and all that stemmed from Shiki. It was his idea—and an extraordinary idea, really—that a haikuist could write virtually a long poem if he worked sequentially. That was Shiki's invention, and as I say in my introduction of *Cage of Fireflies*, it was the result, in large part, of Shiki's reading of and appreciation of modern poetry in other languages, principally English. He was very much aware of what was going on, and he wanted to give haiku the possibility of rendering such complexity that only a longer poem, perhaps, could bring to any subject.

We wonder about that at times, of course, those of us who love haiku and either write it or translate it, because we feel that with a haiku, as an isolated moment, it is everything. When I read Boncho, for example, that poem I always quote and love so much:

Permissions pending.

With something like that I think he said it *all*. On the other hand, we know what Shiki had in mind when he thought of rensaku, sequential composition. That was bound to lead to his feeling that the poet had to be free, that he could abandon structures. He went on to say that nevertheless, in spite of perhaps using 18 syllables, or 16 syllables, or 19—whatever—there still should be seasonal reference, and there should be unity, and in such statements he was echoing Basho. Basho said all that, of course. I think that all the aesthetic statements made—the good ones—are echoes of Basho. Basho said them first and said them best.

ELLIOTT: It was interesting that you had Shiki say in that dialogue of yours, "Come, Basho, you know full well you are regarded as Japan's greatest poet."[2]

STRYK: And he is. Every poet I have ever spoken with in Japan—Takahashi, for example—thinks that Basho is the greatest Japanese poet. Now that surprises some American critics and poets because they might not be aware of the great esteem in which Basho is held.

ELLIOTT: Was that something you were imagining Shiki would say, or did he in fact say that in some context?

STRYK: No, that is imaginary, based on his remorse toward the end of his life over the boldness of some of his comments. He felt guilty and stupid. That is true; he did say *that*. But at the same time, how could he *not* have known? Everyone feels that. Talk with any scholar, any good living poet, they all point to Basho; and if one reads him, and particularly reads him in the original, there is no question. It is the densest, the most subtle, the most moving of all poetry in the form.

ELLIOTT: How do you mean the densest?

STRYK: In some of his poems, the complexity is so great. To hold that much in 17 syllables is a miracle. You get that in the other haikuists, of course, but not as frequently and not quite as densely. Occasionally you do. We shouldn't overstate here, and perhaps I am to a degree. In my experience as a translator, I would say he is the hardest to translate. That's another way of putting it.

ELLIOTT: One thing I've always wondered about Basho is to what degree some of the qualities that make him so highly regarded in Japan are ones you really need to know the language to appreciate. For example, is Basho a poet who is well known for the sound quality of his poems?

STRYK: Yes, absolutely. Sam Hamill has a very good essay in *Basho's Ghost* in which he makes an analysis of a Basho poem based on sound. It's very good, one of the best paragraphs or so that I have read on Basho. It's because he analyzes sound values, and he says, quite rightly—this has always been my thought—that for some reason people in the West who care for haiku think that sound value is not important. They are wrong. It's extremely important.

ELLIOTT: That is perhaps because so much of their introduction to it is in translation. Although translators are probably trying to make as good a poem in English as they can, the sound values may be the most difficult aspect of a poem to carry over into a translation. That's an example of what I meant at the beginning of our conversation when I was talking about sacrifices. Do you feel that in your translation of Basho, for example, you are trying to approach his subtlety of sound?

STRYK: Absolutely. That's what makes him so difficult. And I think I am as much conscious of sound value when working on a Basho poem as when doing one of my own poems. I don't know how I can put that any better, because I am as equally conscious of the need to bring into the translation the sound of the poem and the impact in translation.

ELLIOTT: Another element of poetry that readers are never sure they are getting in a translation is syntax, and of course, Japanese is so different from English.

STRYK: Now there, of course, is exactly the problem in translation, and that is where the poet, given his lights, given his capacities, must take liberties, must pull and wrench apart syntax. He uses the syntax which, at the same time, captures the spirit, the sound of the original. If you were to see, word for word, the structure of, say, the original Basho, I think you'd be often surprised, but I think when the translation is good, you would be pleased as well that the poet has taken that kind of trouble. There is a twist, a turn. There has to be.

ELLIOTT: How would you compare the translating of Issa to the translating of Basho?

STRYK: Basho by far is the more difficult for the reasons I've given, though there are many Issa poems which have great subtlety and certainly great depth. But by and large, he is more idiomatic. What is the difference between Dylan Thomas and Robert Frost, for example? That's the way you might think of them. I don't mean Basho would have the kind of absolutely free spirit you would find in a Dylan Thomas or Hart Crane, poets whose work is so dense and so bold in syntax and word choice, but he is much closer than Issa would be. Issa surprises us (and this is why he is such a great poet) with his insight, with his compassion:

Permissions pending.

Extraordinary! How many people feel these things?

Permissions pending.

That's marvelous! What a world he brings into such art. You see, that is what Issa does over and over again, but he does it through that wonderfully compassionate spirit, which is not absent in Basho, but it is not the whole thing in Basho; there is the poet manipulating sound. He is in language often far more brilliant—more consciously the poet. But never too consciously the poet.

ELLIOTT: If an analogy between Basho and Dylan Thomas is valid, I tend to think of Issa more like a William Carlos Williams.

STRYK: Maybe so. Maybe so. That's good. Except that I think, given Williams's choice of method, you find many prosy patches. I don't mean to use the word in any derogatory sense here. It is the nature of his poetry. We like him for it, and I have great admiration for him, but that's the way it is. That isn't true of Issa, of course; in that small space you can't be. You can't be prosy in haiku. But Williams did allow himself in many of

147

his poems that kind of stretch. Eventually we come to these marvelous moments, but there is that prosiness.

ELLIOTT: Could you talk about your desire to translate the other two of "the great four" [Basho, Buson, Issa, and Shiki]?

STRYK: Yes, I have that desire. It's even amusing to me actually why I have the temerity to set myself such a goal, but as a translator of haiku that has been my goal, to do the four, the great four. It takes me a long time to move toward each of them. Shiki will not be the problem for me, I believe, that Buson will be. Not a problem exactly, except I see in Buson the possibilities of a very unique book that will take a lot of time to plan, loving his painting as much as I do. And I don't mean by that slapping a haiku next to any old painting. I mean judging the quality of each in finding, almost calibrating, the subtleties that would make them wonderful companions on facing pages. More than one poem, perhaps. That's the book I would love to do, because I have such a great love for Buson as a painter, and that whole school, the Literati school. You remember the Taiga scroll on the cover of my *Collected Poems*. He was Buson's great companion, and they did that wonderful group of paintings together. One is on *Cage of Fireflies* from the collection, "Juben Ju-gi" that they collaborated on in 1771. That is one of them, and the Buson are like that. That would be a remarkable book, but it would take a lot of time, and I can't imagine spending time in a better way. But it is for that reason that I have hesitated with the Buson. I have a lot of his pieces already, but I need many more. I can't imagine doing such a book with fewer than 250 or 300 poems. I don't want to do a lesser book. Both the Basho and the Issa have about two or three hundred. The Issa, as you might have noticed, has a rather unique structure. Of course it's seasonal, but it also has 366 pieces because the year of the publication was a leap year, so that was calculated. The divisions are not precise, but I wanted to give the sense of the year.

ELLIOTT: Like *A Year of My Life*.

STRYK: That's right. But the Basho has about 250. That is about one-fourth of his output. And the Buson would have to have that many. That's a lot, when you consider I want a number of them to be pieces others have not translated.

ELLIOTT: I have a question with regard to Basho's output. When you say roughly 1,000 . . .

STRYK: That doesn't include the poems in the haibun, of course. When we speak of 1,000 haiku, we have to bear in mind the haibun as well.

ELLIOTT: Yes, with haiku embedded in them. Does that count of 1,000 also include links found in renga?

STRYK: No. Those who speak of his output do not consider the links of renga. They do not consider them as a discrete haiku.

ELLIOTT: Just the hokku, the first one?

STRYK: Exactly. From there on, links, or variations on—whatever you'd like to call them.

ELLIOTT: Having translated other Japanese poetry—Takahashi, for example, which must be quite difficult—do you find that haiku is even more difficult to translate?

STRYK: Much more difficult. Look at what you are trying to do with so few words. When I translate Takahashi it's difficult enough, of course, but then I can work more as a modern poet. I'm comfortable with the structure of his poems; I'm comfortable with their freedom. There are always problems, but there are far fewer. The greatest problems I have ever had have been with Basho. Some of the classic Zen poems have given me perhaps equal difficulty. But there, you see, something else happens. The difference between my translations of classic Zen poetry and of the great masters in haiku is this: in this case of the Zen poetry, I am working with principles. There are certain things each poem would attempt to convey—whether a satori poem, or a death poem—that are very clear conceptually. I have the advantage of knowing that the poet was struggling with something like a particular element of Zen practice, a particular concept related to Zen thought, so my path is clear. When I get the poem right, that thing will be made clear.

Now, with haiku that doesn't happen. And in my introduction to *On Love and Barley: Haiku of Basho*, by the way, I speak of that. I give three or four poems by Dōgen, the great Zen master, and contrast them to a few poems by Basho in which he had no thought of concepts or anything else, and I make the claim for the haiku, that in spite of all that, they contain that wisdom, the same amount of wisdom.

ELLIOTT: You must be familiar with the book, *One Hundred Frogs*. It certainly raises questions about translation when it presents 100 versions (actually I think there are more than 100) of Basho's famous frog haiku. Again, with regard to what translators are willing to either sacrifice or make allowances for, this author, Hiroaki Sato, tries to make the case that translations of haiku should be one line.

STRYK: I'm not interested in him for that reason.

ELLIOTT: Is it not the case that they are printed that way in the original Japanese?

STRYK: Of course, but that's not the point. You can't render them properly.

ELLIOTT: What is your justification for putting them in three lines?

STRYK: The fact is that we, as English speaking poets, can get said what we feel the haiku really wants us to get said in three lines. It's the nature of our language and it's the nature of our poetry in English to work stanzaically. That's the simplest and best way. I know that Sato is a serious gentleman and he is doing what he feels he must do, but I'm just not comfortable with it. Others may be, but I do not feel I am reading haiku when I read his one-liners, whereas in the original I am.

ELLIOTT: Is it because, at least for someone familiar with haiku in Japanese, when you read the one line, the three-part division is clearly manifest?

STRYK: Of course, it's manifest.

ELLIOTT: In a way that in one-line translations in English it is not?

STRYK: That's right, not in English, because of the cutting words, the kireji, and so on. In Japanese, it's obvious; that's the way they're done. When we're trying to convey them to people, to readers who have no awareness of that, we must, in order to get the kind of impact we feel the poem needs, resort to the three lines. Why have our best translators in haiku (many of whom are as much aware as Hiroaki Sato of the Japanese) elected to use the three-line form from Blyth on? That's the reason.

Now that is about as far as I would like to go. I have no criticism, and obviously he is a very serious worker in the field and his words on the art have to be taken seriously. It is his practice that I'm concerned about. I have to respond as forthrightly as possible in a discussion of this kind, and I'm also aware of something else. I do not wish to give any suggestion to readers, who might be wondering about the nature of this art and wondering about what they are getting from translation, that there is a better way than the way most of us are translating. I am among those who feel that the structure we've arrived at—all the way back, whether you speak of Blyth or Henderson or so many others—is the proper one. I also have reservations about some of the work done in the tercet form. For example, I am not at all convinced by Henderson's rhyming.

ELLIOTT: Do you think he just wants to add another dimension that is conventional in English?

STRYK: He says so. What he says, he makes sound rather convincing. I think he was really doing what he thought was necessary, but I am not convinced. I find many of his translations are embarrassing.

ELLIOTT: Of these 100 versions of the frog haiku, yours is one of the shorter ones, and in general, your translations are on the lean side, compared with even Blyth, who doesn't try to add up to 17 syllables. What sort of rationale have you reached for being on that end of the spectrum?

STRYK: That's the way the original comes at me, with the impact. Any more language would lessen the impact. That's all; that's the only reason. You have to understand that what I'm rendering there is what I wish the English-speaking reader could receive from that poem. That's it. I'm not making any claims for it; I am not claiming it is better than other translations. That's not the point. It's the way I must translate it. But if you look at my other translations you'll find a similar kind of thing happening. That's why Makoto Ueda, for example, who knows my translations, feels I translate as a Zennist. And he's right. But when I say that, I make no excuses. That's the way my eye moves and my senses absorb the original.

May I add one thing to our discussion of the frog pond poem? I know why it's discussed as much as it is. In one of the interviews in Susan

Porterfield's book, *Zen, Poetry, The Art of Lucien Stryk*, the interviewer asked me about that and said something like, *Isn't it symbolic?* and I responded to his question, saying yes, it is symbolic but not metaphorical, and it is utterly true to the act of the frog's leaping. It's a very important poem in Japan too, of course. It's thought of in the same way. It's a very important haiku because of what it started, but I do not think it's his greatest achievement as a haikuist.

ELLIOTT: Anyone who teaches poetry knows that there is often a distinction between great poems and those poems that you have to teach because they are important. They are great in their importance, but they may not be the best poems.

STRYK: Exactly. It is by no means as wonderful as some of the others, but it is, of course, a strong poem. And then we have the many takeoffs on that poem, such as Sengai's, and many allusions to it.

ELLIOTT: I was very interested in the comment you made about Issa where you said that although he was not a Zen Buddhist, the influence of Basho carried with it the Zen element, which had simply become an identifying characteristic of haiku.

STRYK: Yes, all-permeating. I believe that most firmly. That is the reason why, when Takashi Ikemoto and I sat down and began working on *The Penguin Book of Zen Poetry*, I came to him with the idea of including haiku, as he says in his note on our translation at the front of the book. It was my idea, and I said to him exactly what I said in the passage that you alluded to a moment ago. It was by no means an easy decision. Since Basho, I think, it can be claimed that haiku is really a Zen art, and D. T. Suzuki said as much. I think we had every right to include a section of haiku in spite of the fact that a number of poets could not have thought themselves Zennists.

ELLIOTT: You have said that when translating Takahashi, you chose, in at least one instance, to delete some words, with his approval. In a couple of the Issa and Basho haiku I was able to get a translation of, you sometimes make that choice with regard to haiku, which is one of the ways you render them leaner.

STRYK: That's right; it does happen, I admit. You have to bear in mind, and I say as much in everything I've written on my work as a translator, that I have always submitted my poems to the expert judgment of my Japanese friends and collaborators. I would not have dared to present these poems without some kind of authorization. I've always thought of it as a kind of authorization. I work on my own, then submit my work to the very fine judgements of Takashi Ikemoto and of Noboru Fujiwara. In the case of Fujiwara, he was a very fine haiku poet, a Tenro haikuist. Ikemoto was almost a case apart. He was a remarkable Zennist, very sensitive to all the arts associated with Zen. This is what I am leading to. I have never yet presented a poem in haiku translation which I felt was lacking the essential of the original. Of course, I wouldn't have dared to.

ELLIOTT: Are you familiar with this book? [*Snow Falling from a Bamboo Leaf: The Art of Haiku*, by Hiag Akmakjian] It's one of the few I own that has what appears to be a word-for-word English transliteration down at the bottom of the page, below his translation, like a trot. I don't know Japanese, of course, but looking at these I can see what you would be working with in terms of the units of information that are given in the Japanese and what order they are given in. With regard to a couple of the Basho and Issa poems, I was wondering if you might talk about some of the choices you made, starting with the leaping frog poem. You are one of the few translators in that collection of 100 who reversed the second and third units:

> Old pond,
> leap-splash
> —a frog. [5]

What made you feel that putting the frog as the last element rather than the water sound was somehow more appropriate?

STRYK: Greater impact. It's an arguable point, but particularly in the case of that poem, I just felt it that way. I think the great surprise was the frog. There is always "sound of water." Anything could have made it, you see: a stone tossed in, a branch falling. It's a frog. That's the way I see it. Granted, that may be a rather special, an unusual reading, but that's the way I see it, and I think it is a good translation.

ELLIOTT: Do you pay any attention to other people's translations?

STRYK: It's always after the fact, and perhaps never. I never look at other translations, consciously. For example, I might have been scared off doing what I did in my translation by all the voluminous literature related to and translations of that poem. Who am I? [Laughing.] I tend to be unashamedly bold about such things. Again, I am not claiming and would never dare claim that my translations are superior to those of others. That's not the point. But I think you will find in my translations from book to book that there is a consistency. When you read all of the Basho done in *On Love and Barley*, I think you may find (I hope this is true) a voice (I'm not saying it's Basho's voice, or course) rather in the way when you read Basho in the original you find a distinctive voice. Now if that voice, the voice heard by the reader, has sufficient feeling or is sufficiently convincing, then at least some experience will be had. Beyond that I would not wish to say, would have no right to say.

ELLIOTT: Here's another one, a rather famous one, the crow on the branch:

> On the dead limb
> squats the crow—
> autumn's night. [6]

Other translations that I'm familiar with translate the very last word in the poem as either "evening" (Akmakjian[7] Aitkin[8] Ueda[9] and Blyth[10]) or "nightfall" (Henderson[11]) and you have just flat out, "night." Is the Japanese word ambiguous enough that it suggests a range of daylight?

STRYK: It's night to my ears and my eyes. I think the other two are a bit too fanciful, or would be for me. It is not evening. "Evening" doesn't have the color of "night." What's the other word?

ELLIOTT: "Nightfall."

STRYK: Why nightfall? Night. That is a crow; it has solidity, a terseness. That's what I want.

ELLIOTT: And then the choices for what the crow is doing: one says "settles" (Alanakjian), one says "has settled" (Henderson), one says "perched" (Blyth), two say "is perched" (Ueda and Aitken), and for you it "squats."

STRYK: You see, what I am after is this. Obviously it would have had to perch to be on the branch. I want the sense of the crow on that branch, already there, and to me that's what it would be: "squats." "Settles" is if you see it landing, and if you do that you cannot possibly have at the same time a sense of night, the solidity of that blackness. So it's in that way that, throughout my work as a translator, I suppose, I work—to give that sensation. The translator who uses "perched" is, in my judgement, not giving as solid a sense of the sensation. But it's again so hard. I should be a bit cautious here. I can only say that that's the way I see the poem.

ELLIOTT: I thought that Issa's "world of dew" poem was a good example of your bare bones approach. As I can understand it from the English transliteration here, Issa does repeat the phrase "world of dew" twice, but you have it said once, which I think works very well.

STRYK: And then I say, "Perhaps, /and yet . . . " I think that gives the greater sense of what Issa feels. I think anyone coming onto the poem, perhaps for the first time, unaware of the many, many things which have been written about it, reading it the way we most often find it, would not quite get the reason for the repetition. It might not mean to such a reader what in fact I believe my version suggests. It needn't *say* the repetition. I find Issa in a far more seriously reflective mood that way:

Permissions pending.

Whereas, "World of dew / world of dew / and yet" wouldn't quite do that. Do you see the subtleties? That's the kind of thing one is always involved in, working in haiku.

ELLIOTT: When I look at the exact transliteration into English, I see what the translator is up against because of the differences between the languages: "World of dew as for / world of dew yet / however." It's such a different language from English. I was also interested in a comparison of your translation to Issa's poem about not killing the fly. Apparently, word for word, it says
Permissions pending.
(eliminating grammatical function words). And yet "wring its hands," in your version, is obviously the way to say it in English:

155

Permissions pending.

STRYK: Yes, but that's the way we see it, not only in English; that's in fact what happens.

ELLIOTT: What has been happening to haiku in Japan during the last 40 years? Is haiku, as far as you can tell, as vital as it has been in the past?

STRYK: I think not, from what I have been told, not quite. Now Fujiwara would often tell me about this. You get a sense of that perhaps in *Encounter with Zen*, when I speak with a few of the Zennists who write haiku. The conflicts, as between Soun and Tenro schools and so on, have been much discussed. The poets are very much aware of different schools—a kind of factionalism. Seishi, when I last heard, was still alive, a very old gentleman. I hope he is, but I'm not sure; he probably isn't. Fujiwara thought he was the last of the great haiku poets, and some of the others I have spoken with have told me that.

ELLIOTT: An issue that is sometimes discussed in the contemporary American haiku community is whether a season word is essential. Of course, one of the things that is pointed out is that, because we are such a large country, regional seasonal words don't necessarily have the same meaning for people who are from other parts of the country, and so on. I'm not sure how valid that is. But how essential an element do you think those kigo are?

STRYK: Seasons should be suggested somehow, but it doesn't need a word, one word, to suggest season. In Japanese there is the kigo, but some sense of whatever is happening in the haiku, whatever is shown, should suggest at the same time a season in which the event or the thing occurs. Perhaps it's the nature of the Japanese language; perhaps it's because of the expectations readers have. They look for it; they want season; they find it. I'm not sure why. But it's always part of it, as Shiki himself said it should be.

ELLIOTT: Does the post-Shiki Soun school tend to be more liberal with regard to season words?

STRYK: Yes, much more liberal, with almost everything and with season words as well.

ELLIOTT: So they would go beyond Shiki, even though they claim him as their inspiration.

STRYK: They would go beyond him and they are, in fact, not appreciated by all. Fujiwara dismissed them, saying they're just free versers, that's all. [Laughing.]

ELLIOTT: I'd like to raise a question (which I believe was also raised in the Porterfield book) about your feelings on writing original haiku in English. I know you don't do it yourself, and one of the things you've said is you have such a high estimation of classical haiku that you feel you don't want to find yourself coming up short.

STRYK: Yes, I think I've said I've tried and have found myself coming up short. [Laughing.] I haven't liked what I've done; it just hasn't been good enough. Though I think I qualified that when I said in the interview with Kent Johnson that they might have been seen as publishable, but that's what I felt. What I find in these originals is so startling, so remarkable, that nothing I attempted approached that quality. Hence I didn't want to commit myself as an original writer of haiku.

ELLIOTT: Do you think in any way that it has to do with the nature of English? I heard someone once express the opinion that haiku was so inherently Japanese, linguistically, that . . .

STRYK: I don't think so, because good haiku are being written. I read many that I like very much. It's not that; it's a personal thing. Oh no, I have no problem with reading haiku done by English or American poets. Some are very good. I enjoy them very much. On the other hand, to be asked whether I think they are as good as Basho or something is not the point. I don't think it's a question that should be asked. But I think they are good. Most recently at the Midwestern Haiku Conference, where I gave a talk, I found some pieces which pleased me very much. I was able to talk with poets. There was even a kind of workshop where I was shown things. It was very good. To say the least, I approve. It's just that I, myself, have been unable to come up with haiku I thought would be good enough.

ELLIOTT: With regard to your not having written haiku, it does seem, though, going through your work, that it's almost as if haiku are embedded in them.

STRYK: That's exactly right. I think if you take *Of Pen and Ink and Paper Scraps*, there are so many examples. Let me, if I may, give you the start of the first stanza of one or two poems where perhaps it is quite clear that the influence is there. For example, "Dreaming to Music." This is the first stanza:

Permissions pending.

That's the first stanza of the poem. Or the first part of "Wind Chime," actually only a line and a half: Permissions pending. That could be taken from a haiku. Throughout the book, so many moments, so many moments, and some maybe even more obvious than those.

ELLIOTT: Those are the type of things I had in mind.

STRYK: Yes, throughout my work, this happens all the time and in poems that I'm sure you know, like "Zen: The Rocks of Sesshu." And you might remember in the essay, which Susan Porterfield brought into her book, *Making Poems*, I speak of making that poem.

ELLIOTT: Yes, stanza by stanza.

STRYK: I call them "image units," a rather fanciful term for stanza, perhaps, but I thought of them as that, and to many who know that poem well, they read very much like haiku. There is no question the influence is still there in many of the new poems I'm doing. "The Round" is a piece which may suggest well the way in which my work as a translator of haiku has affected my own writing:

> Slowly, dark through
> the sycamore shadows
>
> the window, fuzzes wind-
> dodging birds set down

in its branches. I listen
in wonder to icicles

chiming night rituals of
winter. Wait for dawn's

whirl-spin of light
and the shiver of wings.[17]

So there I think I'm writing a poem which I don't think I would have written
had I not translated many haiku. That represents for me the richness of
my experience as translator. One works in mysterious ways. I don't deny
or would wish to deny—in fact I'm very happy about the fact—that the
evidence is in my poetry. That's of course what I hope. Just as I've always
hoped that the evidence of my work in Zen is in my life.

ELLIOTT: Where else?

STRYK: Where else? That's right.

ELLIOTT: Do you feel at all uncomfortable being identified as a poet who
has found Zen and Buddhism important?

STRYK: No, but on the other hand, I don't like being categorized. I would
rather not be thought of as a Zen poet, one reason being it goes so much
against the grain of Zen experience. A man with no title is my ideal.
But I would hate to feel that someone coming on to my poetry would
immediately perceive things as indentifiably Zen, which would, for such a
reader, represent a lesser reading experience, more limited.

ELLIOTT: One might think that that's the sole key to open it up.

STRYK: Yes, and it isn't at all. Poems which may best reflect my involvement
in Zen thought usually have nothing ostensibly there as Zen. The poems
are written in my back yard or wherever.

ELLIOTT: Ordinary mind.

Stryk: Ordinary mind, that's right, exactly. In fact one of my poems is called "The Ordinary," in my *Collected Poems*. So I can become uncomfortable when people call me a Zen poet. Or if they pick up my book, a book like my *Collected* and start looking for evidence of it. Fortunately, I think, the best of the people who have written on my work have not been of that kind. If anything, even in a review that appeared of my *Collected*, in *Library Journal*, the reviewer was good enough to say that what he thought was most interesting is the way in which I seem to have incorporated those things in my life, or brought them into my life and hence could write about all sorts of things without wanting to be seen as a Zen poet.

Notes

[1] Lucien Stryk, *Cage of Fireflies: Modern Japanese Haiku*, Swallow Press, Athens, Ohio (1993), p. 5.

[2] Stryk, *Cage of Fireflies*, p. 16.

[3] Stryk, *The Dumpling Field: Haiku of Issa*, Swallow Press, Athens, Ohio (1991), p. 8.

[4] Stryk, *The Dumpling Field*, p. 6.

[5] Stryk, *On Love and Barley: Haiku of Basho*, Penguin Books, New York (1985), p. 58.

[6] Stryk, *On Love and Barley*, p. 35.

[7] Hiag Akmakjian, *Snow Falling from a Bamboo Leaf: The Art of Haiku*, Capra Press, Santa Barbara, California (1979), p. 48.

[8] Robert Aitken, *A Zen Wave: Basho's Haiku & Zen*, Weatherhill, New York (1978), p. 28.

[9] Makoto Ueda, *Matsuo Basho*, Kodansha, Tokyo (1982), p. 44.

[10] R.H. Blyth, *Haiku Vol. 3*, Hokuseido Press, Tokyo (1952), p. 338.

[11] Harold G. Henderson, *An Introduction to Haiku: An Anthology of Poems and Poets from Basho to Shiki*, Doubleday Anchor, Garden City, New York (1958), p. 18.

[12] Stryk, *On Love and Barley*, p. 35.

[13] Stryk, *The Dumpling Field*, p. 105.

[14] Stryk, *The Dumpling Field*, p. 15.

[15] Stryk, *Of Pen and Paper Scraps*, Swallow Press, Athens, Ohio (1989), p. 10.

[16] Stryk, *Of Pen and Ink and Paper Scraps*, p. 15.

[17] Stryk, *Where We Are: Selected Poems and Zen Translations*, London, Skoob Books, London (1996), by permission of Lucien Stryk and Skoob Books.

IX. Praise Is a Generative Act

A Conversation with Pattiann Rogers

Scranton, Pennsylvania
November 1995

Pattiann Rogers (b. 1940) is the author of 12 books of poetry, including *Song of the World Becoming: New and Collected Poems, 1981-2001*. She has taught at several universities including the University of Arkansas and Pacific University.

ELLIOTT: The world of scientific knowledge is so present in your work that I would like to know if you have any sort of academic background in science.

ROGERS: When I was an undergraduate I had an equal interest in zoology and English literature. I took a minor in zoology. Before I made that decision, I was considering whether I would major in zoology or English literature. When it came time to make the decision, and I realized that if I majored in zoology I wouldn't be able to take any more literature courses, that made me sad and I realized English literature was probably the major I needed to choose. The minor in zoology gave me enough of a background to know where to go to look for information if I needed it. Also, the Bachelor of Arts required a number of hours in a physical science. I had a five-hour course in astronomy at the University of Missouri. It was a lecture course that met one hour a day all five days of the school week for an entire semester. It was a thorough course. It also had an element of ritual to it, in that the class met at 1:00 in the afternoon, so every afternoon at the same time I would walk across the campus, the bells would begin to chime, and I would walk into the Physics building, up the stairs, into the lecture hall, and to my seat.

Dr. Schopp was the professor, and his lectures were just elevating to me. It was like being released, a liberation. He was a professor who loved his subject, who was capable of bringing it to a level of undergraduate work, and I thought the details of that science were fascinating. Those two things, the minor in zoology and the astronomy course, profoundly affected me. And then my husband is a physicist. He has a Ph.D in physics and so does my older son. They have been a source of conversation on this subject. I've been allowed into the kind of discussion that goes on among scientists, and I have been able to understand their interests in art too.

ELLIOTT: What were your intentions in attempting to draw from the world of science in your poetry?

ROGERS: Both the process of science and the information gathered through science were fascinating to me. I wanted to try to convey that fascination in my poetry. That was one thing I consciously wanted to try to do. I thought scientific research was exhilarating. Also, I knew there was a scientific vocabulary that hadn't been tapped, an evocative, musical, beautiful vocabulary, and I knew it had potential for poetry. I wanted to try to find a way to incorporate that vocabulary into my work, not as something sterile and not as imposed on something else, but as the body out of which imagery and feelings arise.

ELLIOTT: Your first book, *The Expectations of Light*, contains quite a variety of work, even including a few rather uncharacteristic poems that appear to be about relatives. Was it during the writing of that book that you felt you really came to your true subject matter?

ROGERS: Yes. I said earlier that I knew there was one thing I wanted to do and that was to try to express the exhilaration I felt with some of the things science was telling us and to tap into that scientific vocabulary, but every time I tried it, prior to that book, the voice was not right. I knew I was still outside the language. I hadn't achieved the right stance towards the material. I didn't know how to do that.

While I was in the writing program at the University of Houston, I began to write poems that felt as if I were beginning to address what I wanted to address, and it turned out that subject was not just science, of course; it was the questions to which science always leads: ·What are we doing here? Who are we? What is this that is all around us? What do these words "universe" and "God" mean? What's death? What's life? These are the questions science is dealing with too, and so those were the questions that began to develop in the poems.

I can identify the first poem where I came close to doing what I had been trying to do for a long time, and that's "The Rites of Passage." It's in *The Expectations of Light* and *Firekeeper*. It is the poem about the development of frog eggs (well, the ostensible subject). That was something I'd experienced in my zoology class. I worked with tadpole eggs with a professor of embryology and watched their development. Another experience that informed that poem happened when I was a teenager after we had moved to a farm. I remember the image I saw when I held in my hand a broken egg that a hen had laid. It was a fertilized egg, and the embryo had begun to develop. I was holding half the egg, and in the center was a dot of blood. Radiating out from that dot were what looked like small arteries or veins, and the center dot was pulsing. It was a surprising kind of thing to see. I remembered that, and it was part of the impetus of that poem, "The Rites of Passage." I was able to draw on that experience and on my experience with the frog eggs to address something else. When is that beginning moment of life? When does the moment occur when prior there was no life and then there is life, and what are the ramifications of that life coming into being?

I wrote that poem, and I remember then being almost in a panic that I wasn't going to be able to do it again, that I was going to forget how I achieved that tone and stance I needed. So for a long time I was afraid *not* to write. I felt that I had to write as fast as I could, because if I didn't I would forget, like swimming up stream; if you stop swimming you're going to be carried back down where you were. So I kept writing as fast as I could, trying to achieve that same opening that would allow me to go where I wanted to go.

ELLIOTT: Is there an intended connection between the form of some of your poems and the scientific method? A number of them read like what physicists talk about as "thought experiments."

ROGERS: Yes. That is true, especially in *The Expectations of Light*. The structure of many of the poems consists of suppositions: "Imagine that things are like this," or "Suppose it's like this." That is the way scientists talk so often, and it's the way Einstein laid out many of his thought experiments. Einstein rode a trolley from work at the patent office in Zurich and he could see the clock in the tower and he thought, What if I was riding on the beam of light coming from that clock? What would happen to time? How would time appear to me? That notion of supposing, of thought experiments, is a structure that I used. I didn't know I was doing that, but it was the approach that scientists take to a problem. I believe it was Einstein who said that what we do as scientists is to try to construct a garment and then hold it up to the universe to see if it fits. I guess it can be said that a poem is written like that, too: suppose these things and suppose these things, and then hold the poem up and see if it fits anything, or perhaps see if the design of the poem illuminates a design in nature.

ELLIOTT: Do you perceive any parallels between the way you structure poems and the way the natural world or the cosmos is structured?

ROGERS: That's a fascinating question to me. It would please me to think that some of the poems operate in that way. I do believe that images in the natural world are potential sources for determining the form the poem takes. The branches of a tree suggest connections, linguistic connections, as do the spirals of a conch shell, the helix of DNA, the layering of the petals of a rose, the building of clouds, the rising of smoke. All of these natural images are models for the way language can build, link, branch, expand, turn around itself. I address this thought in "The Mad Linguist," in which I suppose that the structure of language has been built around patterns that we see in nature or motions that we see in nature.

ELLIOTT: Poetry about nature has, of course, been written in strict, traditional forms, but I was wondering if perhaps you felt that your leaning toward more organic, open forms (free verse but still with a very discernible structure, some sort of incremental repetition, for example, a combination of structure and openness) was in any way mirrored your vision of the way form manifests itself in nature.

ROGERS: I would love for that to be true. I think that I will say two things about this. One is that we cannot separate ourselves from nature, and whatever we do in some sense is linked to it because our bodies are part of the physical world. Even dividing things into physical and spiritual is artificial. So even traditional forms must have their replication somewhere in nature, either in the way we are moving or speaking or in fixed patterns. I did write in traditional forms for a long time. In fact I have a small chapbook of poems that are in traditional forms, in meter, full rhymes, sonnets, other fixed forms.

ELLIOTT: This was before the poems in *The Expectations of Light*?

ROGERS: Yes. I thought, like many people still think, that it was cheating, it wasn't really poetry if you didn't adhere to some fixed form that regulated for you the length of your lines, that prescribed for you a rhyming scheme. I scanned my lines for regularity of accented and unaccented syllables and adhered to meter.

ELLIOTT: Do you now feel that your early work in closed forms was valuable in any way?

ROGERS: I think it made me aware of the metrics of language. Whether I actually scan my work or not now, I think that I am aware of how the accents are falling and how the music is determined by the meter, or the lack of it, or the rhythm, the cadence. I think too that the sounds—rhyming and alliteration and assonance—are there. In fact, many of my poems have rhymes in them. They just aren't at the ends of the lines.

To think of form in poetry as only meter and rhyme or regularity of stanza construction (although these can be important formal elements) now seems to me restrictive and lacking in imagination. And to believe that the forms that have satisfied the aesthetic needs and considerations of people of other times can also meet the aesthetic needs and requirements of our time seems to me a limited and ultimately dissatisfying approach to creating poetry, or, for that matter, any art. The form of our writing must allow us to address the questions and dilemmas crucial to our time, and address them in the very unique ways in which they reveal themselves to us. This means creating forms, cadences, and patterns of sound that enable and release thought and emotion.

Form must be integral to the many different circumstances of our times. The form of the poem will rise from the experiences and concerns of each individual writer, of course. But we are all affected to some degree by the tempo and patterns and cadences we live with, not just by the music we hear, but by the way we weave in and out of crowds of people on a sidewalk, for instance, or on an airport concourse, by our means of moving from one location to another—automobile, bicycle, train—motions which our bodies feel and assimilate constantly.

ELLIOTT: So you feel the forms of your poems are inspired not only by nature but by other experiences.

ROGERS: Yes, we are affected rhythmically and formally by the tools we handle daily, the way our hands are shaped by a doorknob or a faucet, a comb, a fork, by the wheel we grip to determine our direction (that circle turning) , the pedal against the foot and the slowing or accelerating of our bodies, the experience of pressing a button or flipping a switch and seeing, expecting, a certain result from that action. These are such common experiences. We must assume that they are influencing our sense of the movement of time; and the language, the music in a poem is a movement of time. For instance, I did a great deal of sewing by hand when I was young, and I'm certain that the slow, meticulous threading of the needle, the tiny stitches made, the attention to color, and the shape of the color the thread took against the cloth, this careful stitch-by-stitch creation of a vision, has influenced the method I use to construct my poems and thus the resulting forms. This isn't the only source determining the form language assumes in my poetry, but it is one that I believe I recognize.

Even the games we engage in, both currently and in our childhoods—swimming, baseball, jumping rope, for example—have form, divisions based on time and action, pauses and accelerations, regular rhythms. It would be negligent not to suppose that these games in their rhythms and units of action, which have become part of the way we move and organize our thoughts, would not affect to some degree the forms we find aesthetically satisfying in the written language. (I'm not speaking of these activities as *subjects* of poems, but as activities which might influence the music and pattern in any particular poem.)

Visual forms even play a role in the patterns we choose for our language to take. We have images, once again, unique to our times—the image of the earth seen from the moon, the image of sperm squiggling forward, blood corpuscles racing through veins, life and earthforms at the bottom of the sea, computer-generated images, x-rays, photographs of galaxies taken by the Hubble telescope. These images suggest spatial and temporal dimensions, dimensions that I feel should resonate in the language of poetry. Also the speed and manner in which we receive communication, lighted patterns on a screen, computer or television—all of these, and more, are forms, rhythms and patterns that, I believe, affect the choices we make in regard to form in writing, the shape of the time and space and motion we create for our poetry.

But, of course, we also live among cadences common to people of all times—raindrops hitting the earth, the sound of wind in the leaves of a tree in spring or in the dry leaves of a tree in autumn, water rushing over stones, crickets, birds, dogs barking, the silence of snow. Our breath, the beat of our hearts, the pulse as it increases or calms—all of these also are rhythms that will determine, to some extent, the music that pleases us in any given poem.

ELLIOTT: You said earlier that your undergraduate education in science gave you access to material you could use in your poetry. Over the course of your career, have you continued to engage in research, through reading scientific journals, perhaps?

ROGERS: I do not claim to be a mathematician or an astronomer or a zoologist or a geologist. I am not an expert on those subjects. The research I do is not terribly extensive. Sometimes I begin a poem and then realize I need more information; other times I may read something that occasions the poem. It works both ways. For instance, I have a poem called "The Dead Never Fight Against Anything," and much in that poem came from research. I don't remember what occasioned the poem, but I did do research on the various ways that cultures have dealt with the dead, and, of course, like with any research, I was amazed at what I found.

"Infanticide" is another poem very similar in structure. I do know how that poem began. I heard on the news about a newborn baby found in a dumpster. It wasn't dead. It had been turned over to the authorities and they were taking care of it, and I thought I would like to see what part infanticide had played in various cultures and found that it had been a large part of many cultures and was accepted as necessary. Different cultures dealt with it in different ways. So this might not be considered strictly science, the way that physics, astronomy, or zoology are, but the writing of the poem involved research.

ELLIOTT: Well, the same type of intelligence seems to be brought to bear on it. I mean, even though those poems are not scientific so much as anthropological, nevertheless they seem of a piece with most of the rest of your work.

Have you had the opportunity (and perhaps through your husband's colleagues you have, if not in other ways) to discover how scientists reading your poetry would react to it?

ROGERS: Not to the degree I would wish, and that is a disappointment to me, because I would like my work (and I think this is true with every poet) to have a wide audience. I don't want it only to be read by other poets or by people who have degrees in literature, although I love their readership too, but I would love for it to be read by Steven J. Gould, for instance, or my husband's or son's colleagues, and also musicians and people in other fields of art. But many people are afraid of poetry. They don't come to it readily. I think people in other fields, such as science, for example, can appreciate and enjoy music and maybe visual arts, but poetry is something that people don't come to with any kind of eagerness, generally. I think one of the reasons is that it is language used in a way that they are not prepared for. They think that because they can read, and they can read novels and newspapers and textbooks, that language in poetry should be used in the same way. But it isn't at all, and so it irritates some people; it angers some people. If people could think of poetry like music, in that it isn't necessary to make an intellectual translation of it, but that it can be enjoyed for its sound, then it might be more easily appreciated.

Recently I have had the opportunity to give readings to people in a multidisciplinary setting. There have been biologists and people in environmental studies in the audience, and many have come up to me and asked for copies of poems or asked what book a poem is in. That is always gratifying. It pleases me when somebody in a different discipline says to me they like my work. Some of the biologists who have asked for poems have wanted to use them with their students. I think *hearing* the poems has brought people to my work.

I've been able to read to audiences of biologists and environmental scientists as part of "The Forgotten Language Tour." I have done several tours with other writers. The tour is about eleven days long. We go to four or five different campuses in an effort to bring the literature of the natural world to people who are working in the sciences and in environmental studies, because the language they use is often sterile and technical, and yet what drew them into their fields in the first place was the love of the natural world. They will often respond to literature that is celebratory, that tries to express or explore the delight and curiosity we experience in the natural world. The tour is sponsored by the Orion Society. This society also has an educational program for teachers in the summer that focuses on environmental teaching in the classroom, and the society publishes a terrific magazine, a quarterly called *Orion: For Nature and People*.

The term "Forgotten Language" comes from a short poem by Merwin called "Witness":

> I want to tell what the forests
> were like
>
> I will have to speak
> in a forgotten language

How will we know the language of forests if there are no more forests? There is a language of the landscape, and that is what many writers are attempting to capture—the language spoken by the landscape.

ELLIOTT: It seems as if much of your poetry (and this goes back to the remark you made earlier) is, in a sense, trying to reconcile science and faith, maybe increasingly, as I read some of your more recent poems. Is that a justifiable characterization?

ROGERS: I don't know if "reconcile" is the best word. I think that science and faith are both in my work, and I think that the story that science is telling about our surroundings and our beginnings is so much a part of our lives now that to try to shunt it aside and say, "Well, science is over there and faith is over here," is like trying to live a schizophrenic life. Everyone of us accepts at some level the story science tells us. We live by it, it nurtures us, it sustains us. We go to the doctor. The story of our biology we believe, for instance. We have a faith in that; there is a level of faith in it. I wanted to try to tell the story science is telling so that it contained spirituality. The very best scientists see it that way. What was it that the astronomers just saw through the Hubble telescope? They said it was like looking at the face of God.

ELLIOTT: The birth of a planet, wasn't it?

ROGERS: Perhaps the birth of a star. Scientists make statements like these all the time, indicating that their experience is close to a religious experience, that they have a great reverence for the universe. I'm talking about the best scientists, not those who are just technicians, but people who are involved in the metaphysics of the work as well as the physics of it. But there are things that science cannot do and cannot tell us about, and scientists know that, and they don't try to tell us about those things. That is where the responsibility of artists comes in, to both reconcile (and I'll use your word) science to those other needs that we have, reconciling those two things, infusing scientific fact with spirituality. What was it Faulkner said in his acceptance speech? The job of the artist, or he said poet, is to remind people of the glories, honors, and sacrifices of their past, to lift their hearts, and to help them not merely to endure but to prevail. I think it is not the job of science to do that; I agree with Faulkner that it is the responsibility of the artist to attempt to do that. Since this schism is there between art and science, and science and religion, and at the same time our image of ourselves is so influenced by science, it seems to ignore this schism is unhealthy and weakening to people's ability to prevail, to act with generosity and commitment. To try to bridge that schism is important. I hope that other people are attempting to do it too in whatever fields they work in. I've felt from the beginning, that if I could show that it was possible to address scientific issues through poetry and to use the vocabulary of science, then others might come along and do it better than I could.

ELLIOTT: There are people who are writing poems that in certain ways inhabit the same sort of space as yours—Mary Oliver, for example—whose work often seems to be rooted in a very specific geographical location. For Oliver it is Cape Cod. But it is very difficult to say the same thing of your work. I mean, the poems are situated in nature, with many details from the natural world, but as far as a particular locale is concerned, that doesn't seem to be obvious to me. Or is it that I'm just not aware of the particular bioregions you may be drawing from?

ROGERS: No, I think you're right, although I don't think the details are totally out of place either. But identifying a particular region has never been uppermost in my mind. I like drawing attention to the variety of flora, or the possible types of beetles, for instance, the range of individual lives and features, existing in the universe we inhabit. That can be a greater concern to me in any poem than depicting the landscape of Texas or Missouri, for example.

How we perceive, our methods of defining and identifying, and the role that language plays in the processes of the universe have always been uppermost in my mind, and I believe an examination of these processes occurs in many of my poems.

ELLIOTT: In the last year I have seen a couple of your poems in *The Amicus Journal*. You don't address environmental issues overtly, at least from a political standpoint, as Wendell Berry or Gary Snyder sometimes do, but how do you perceive the relationship between your work and environmentalism as a movement?

ROGERS: Many of the "nature writers"—poets, fiction and non-fiction writers—are my very good friends. I support them without hesitation, in every way that I can conscientiously offer my support. And I do believe that the earth, our union with the physical world from which we have come, is central to an understanding of who we are as humans and of what our obligations are. The land, with all of its inhabitants and features, plays a very large role in most of the finest American literature—not only in the work of Whitman, Thoreau, Emerson, Dickinson, but equally in Melville, Twain, Cather, Steinbeck, Faulkner, Hemingway, Roethke. Much of the writing of contemporary "nature writers" is carrying on this tradition of the land being not merely picturesque background or setting, but a source of self-knowledge and sustenance, a force, an actor, often a determining presence in story or poem.

172

I've never regarded my poetry as being overtly or consciously politically charged or directed, in the sense of urging governmental or political or even social action. I've always thought of my poetry as free experimentation with language, an attempt to praise as beautifully and musically as I can those things that I value and that sustain me and give me delight; and as an attempt to articulate areas of experience and feeling not yet articulated, as an effort to expand and refine the definitions of those words that are so vague and yet so important to us—death, love, god, life, honesty, compassion. If a reaffirmation of the importance of the earth and our communion with it emerges from these efforts, then so be it. I'm happy and comfortable with that.

ELLIOTT: You have written a few poems about your family, but not many. Is that a subject matter you would like to do more with? ·

ROGERS: It is troubling to me, because my family has been so important to me. Raising my sons was probably the hardest and most rewarding thing I have ever had to do, hard not in the sense that it was drudgery, but that it was challenging in all ways: intellectually, emotionally, physically. My desire to try to do that job right, to do the best I could at that, took precedence over the writing. There is lack of really good, I mean the best, literature about being a mother. It's just not in the canon.

ELLIOTT: In recent years we have certainly seen an increasing number of dysfunctional families in literature. The challenge is to write poems about functional families.

ROGERS: That's right. Even if you look at Shakespeare, you have Gertrude, a dysfunctional mother in a way to Hamlet; and Lady Macbeth, who we're not sure even had a child. (I guess there is some dispute about that.) Jane Austin's mothers are witless, nervous, sick, weak individuals. Anna Karenina abandons her child. Most of the time it is implied that a mother devoted to her children is some kind of dolt who can't think.

I feel it's imperative that we have strong, beautiful, imaginative writing addressing the intensity of feeling between mother and child. There's no stronger, natural human bond. It's replete with a complexity as wrenchingly human as any subject addressed in our literature.

Until very recently, in the 50's perhaps, most of the women writers represented in our canon were not mothers, beginning with the

Bronte sisters and Jane Austin, up to Emily Dickinson, Virginia Woolf, Willa Cather, Elizabeth Bishop, Marianne Moore, Flannery O'Connor, Eudora Welty, and others. Where is the strong mother's voice, a voice exploring that role, embracing it intellectually and spiritually in the deepest way? It's largely a missing voice that leaves a void in our literary tradition, and it's a voice crucial for the health of the culture, in my opinion.

ELLIOTT: You have one or two poems about sons, but that's about it.

ROGERS: Yes, right. I can see my sons and where they are in my poems and how they influenced my poems, but I don't think anybody else could unless I pointed it out and explained it. To address the family directly, in beautiful, imaginative writing is difficult for me. I don't know how to do it.

This issue is something I'm trying to talk about when I have the opportunity, trying to encourage mothers who are writing to address this subject in the best way they can. Because it is not in the canon, we don't have examples to follow, to learn from, to work against. I have written a couple of essays on this subject. One is in an anthology called *Where We Stand: Women and the Literary Traditions*, published by Norton. The other is in *Orion*.

ELLIOTT: I think of "Finding the Tattooed Lady in the Garden" as being a central poem in your work. Do you agree?

ROGERS: Yes, I do. This poem might be an examination into the way language affects and creates perception and experience. We are creatures of process. We are part of the constant flux and change of the universe, yet we are always seeking the unchanging, a certainty underlying disorder. This seeking takes many forms itself and becomes part of the universe—the arts, science, religion, etc. As part of the universe we are simultaneously affecting and being affected by our surroundings. We know we are not passive, totally hapless creatures. Even as observers, we are affecting what is. Language is an element present in the universe. Once a word is spoken, or even thought, it becomes a part of the universe, a presence that then plays a role in what is and what will be. I address this subject also in "All the Elements of the Scene." The process of engaging the universe in this way—by defining and redefining the eternal, thus experiencing and revising experience and then experiencing the revision—is exhilarating and beautiful. This is the conclusion, I believe, in "Finding the Tattooed Lady in the Garden."

ELLIOTT: I wanted to ask you about a poem you didn't include in *Firekeeper*, "The Literary Man," which seems to say that words create an imaginative reality, but they separate the perceiver from the creation because the language interposes between perceiver and reality, so that you can't see an elm without thinking "elm."

ROGERS: That's right.

ELLIOTT: You project that philosophy onto the man in the poem.

ROGERS: I haven't read that poem in a while, so I'm going to have to think back a little bit, but I'm not sure that the way you characterized it is exactly what I meant. I meant in some ways what you said, that once you see that word it is always there when you see what it correlates to in the world. But at the same time, I don't think that is a negative thing. I don't think it separates, which I know is a Buddhist concept; I think it allows perception. At least this is the theory I work from. Until we can speak about something, we can't really contemplate it. Unless we have language to use for examination, we are blind, handicapped. The first poem in *The Expectations of Light*, "In Order to Perceive," is about that. Until something is pointed out to us, we don't see it, and even if we point it out to ourselves, it is still being pointed out. The way we point it out or distinguish it is to give it a name, give it a word, and then we come to see it. So I think that's part of what the "The Literary Man" is about.

Also, in *Splitting and Binding*, the reason I titled the book that is that I think we are engaged in two functions as human beings, equally valid functions and valuable. One is analysis, in which we take something apart, and then synthesis, in which we put it back together. Part of being human is that continual process of taking apart and then putting back together the world as we come to experience it, to understand it, to revere it. And that very process itself then becomes part of the universe.

ELLIOTT: That reminds me of "Knot."

ROGERS: That is exactly what "Knot" is about. One of our values as human beings is the ability to go back and forth, to analyze, to take apart. We do that with language, and in some sense in the act of doing that, yes, we're separated, but language is also the means by which we put everything back together, too, and enter a richer universe, without separation.

As children we experience a closeness to the earth, we experience *iediately*, without an awareness or examination of our experience, *c*hout a consciousness which allows full appreciation of the experience. *i*s adults we recall those moments of union and attempt to recreate the experience of that immediacy with a cognizance not present in childhood and to celebrate the experience, that facet of our being. Isn't this part of Wordsworth's thinking, "the child is father of the man"?

I'm fond of going to Helen Keller's autobiography and to Anne Sullivan's account of Helen's discovery of language and how that discovery changed her being, even her physical appearance, her face. Helen had never experienced remorse until she gained language. This is an astounding fact. She climbed into her teacher's arms and kissed her on the evening of the day language was revealed to her, the first time she had done this, I believe we begin to create ourselves, our sense of self, what I might call our souls, through language. A poem about this is "Teaching a Sea Turtle Suddenly Given the Power of Language, I Begin By Saying:"

ELLIOTT: Do you ever question the ability of language to live up to your expectations? Much contemporary critical theory posits an inherent inability of language to deliver what we may think it promises in terms of precision or the capacity to express the transcendent.

ROGERS: Everything we do is an approximation. Science is an approximation even. So to think that we are ever going to capture the mystery of this experience of life is foolish. In the end we do what we are capable of doing, knowing that we are ignorant creatures, knowing that our brains rose up in an evolutionary way and are skilled at some things, and not really very skilled at other things and that our brains work in ways we don't understand. For instance, a memory will come racing through our minds and we don't even know why, or what occasioned it. We know that multiple things are going on in our minds all the time. In the end we just do the best that we can do, feeling that somehow we have obligations. At least we . . . let me say "I" as a human creature feel that I have an obligation to give back something for the gift of life, a gift I did nothing to deserve. Any moment of pleasure I have while alive is a pure gift, something I didn't do anything to earn. I think many people feel an obligation to attempt to give something back for the life given. In whatever way we can, we fulfill those obligations, knowing that we imperfectly understand and always will imperfectly understand.

When I am particularly in despair at not being able to formulate exactly what we should be doing here, or what I should be doing, or what life means, or if it looks to me like our existence is an accident, that somehow a creature rose on this planet that was conscious of itself and conscious of the universe, and that was an accident, and we could disappear just like other extinct creatures disappeared and the universe would just go spinning on its way. . . . There are moments when everybody feels that despair, but then I think that perhaps there would be no concept of justice in the universe if it were not for us. Even though we fail at always establishing justice or defining it with ultimate precision, still we have invented a word for a presence not found anywhere else in the universe, that we are aware of. Many of the values we cherish—loyalty, honesty, compassion, generosity—these are human inventions and present in the universe when we practice them. We create them.

And there is one thing we can do that as far as we know no other creature can do, and that is that we can praise. We may not be able to understand the complete mathematics of the stars or the origin of the universe, but we *can* praise. And it is an affirmative act. We know that it generates health somehow. Praise is a generative act because we can feel it when we do it; we can feel the health in our bodies. If we can't do anything else, we can praise and that is one certainty to cling to. It's a certainty *I* cling to.

Notes

Merwin, W. S., "Witness." *The Rain in the Trees*, New York: Knopf, 1988.
    65.
Rogers, Pattiann. *The Expectations of Light*. Princeton, NJ: Princeton
    University Press, 1981.
_____. *Firekeeper*. Minneapolis: Milkweed, 1994.

X. The Complexity of the Human Hear

A Conversation with Marie Howe

La Plume, Pennsylvania
May 2000

(b. 1950) has published four books of poetry, including *What* *)o* and *Magdelene*. She teaches at Sarah Lawrence College, as the Poet Laureate of New York, and is a Chancellor of the American Poets.

ELLIOTT: You started writing poetry seriously somewhat late in life, after taking a summer class at Dartmouth. You have a line in "The Meadow": "As we walk into words that have waited for us to enter them . . . ." Was that the feeling you had at that moment in your life?

HOWE: Don't you feel as if our lives are these compositions that we don't really know how to make end? Every once in a while we walk through a door and we realize, "My God, it's the right door. This is the door I was meant to walk through." I felt that when I took the class at Dartmouth. I was thirty years old, after teaching high school for years and being a journalist, and I felt like this was what I wanted to do. Of course I had doubts. I was beleaguered by doubts, but I had found a joy, and I just felt so happy. It's hard to sustain that over time, of course, because it becomes something else as you look through it and keep going, and your own life takes different turns; but at that period of my life it felt like I had stumbled into the right room and there were clear and specific directions, and I was so, so, so grateful. And the directions were just this kind of profound sense of meaning and happiness in work that meant something to me. I didn't even know I could stay at a desk for five, six hours working on the same thing. So I found a way of being with experience in language that made sense. It was miraculous, looking back at it—a near miss.

ELLIOTT: How long was it until you quit high school teaching after that experience?

HOWE: A year. I went back to school and taught, and I took a workshop in Boston. Then I applied to graduate school and I went the following year.

ELLIOTT: To Columbia?

HOWE: Yes, and I was teaching at Dartmouth. I began teaching at the fellowship program that I had gone to. So I kept going back to New Hampshire for eight summers to teach, even though I was in graduate school, helping adults who come back to school for this master's degree in Liberal Studies. I was there to remind them how to write papers, so I was teaching adult composition, which was great, and then poetry eventually at Dartmouth as well, but high school one more year. I remember late in the fall I said, I could do this seriously. A friend said I should apply to graduate schools, so I began to do that, to put together a group of poems.

I needed ten poems to apply to graduate school, and I think I wrote almost a poem a week for the workshop in Boston, so I had a bunch of poems I was working on. I mean they were nothing I would think about now, but they were a beginning, and I sent them off. Eventually I decided to go to Columbia and did. It was great. I felt like an arrow released from the bow. I really did spout into exactly where I should be. I studied with everybody and took classes in theological school, the literature department . . . I met Stanley Kunitz and he became my friend and teacher. Stanley and I just read together in New York this week, and it was very moving to read with him. I found him my second year of graduate school. What he embodies and how he lives and what his values are in poetry I saw right away and identified with so deeply. Then I gradually got to know him. I was very shy, but I went to his office every week with a new poem. You know, [knocking on table]: "Excuse me, Mr. Kunitz, do you have a minute?" And then I ended up going to the Fine Arts Work Center in Provincetown, which is this wonderful center he founded years ago. So we were able to maintain our friendship, and now it's been a long time and we are good friends, but it was years of [knock, knock] "Excuse me, Mr. Kunitz," before we got to be as close as we are now.

He's amazing. He stays up later than anyone I know. He always outdistances me, every single time. He used to stay at my apartment in Cambridge. Somewhere in the mid-to-late 80s he came to give a reading at Harvard, and I don't know what possessed me; I said, "Do you want to stay with me when you come to Cambridge?" and he said, "I'd love it!" So when he came to Boston to give a reading he would stay at my apartment. I would have a dinner for him, and all of my young poet friends would come and sit around, ten of us, drinking, arguing poetry until two in the morning. Then they would all leave and I would be getting ready to leave to go stay at my boyfriend's and leave Stanley in my room, and he would say, "Now, let's look at some poems!" It's two in the morning! I'm like, "Get out of here! No way!" "Oh come on, let's just look at a couple." It's that Russian peasant blood, I think. I don't know what it is.

ELLIOTT: Is "Part of Eve's Discussion" still a cornerstone poem for you? It seems to establish so effectively the interests that many of your poems have with moments of transformation, of becoming—things on the edge of change.

HOWE: Imminence. When I wrote that it was the first time I was really transported by writing a poem, and it was the first time I found a . . .

"Vehicle" is not the right word; "metaphor" is not quite the right word either. It was a situation that was resonant of some inchoate situation in my own soul. And that situation provided a way of speech, a way of speaking about it, which is for me the struggle in writing. What Frost says, you know, a poem begins with a homesickness, with a lump in your throat and that inchoate homesickness, that gathering of force of new feelings and thoughts. It seems miraculous that it ever finds an expression. And for me it only works one out of thirty times. There are so many poems I throw out, so that Eve poem I think was the first time that something I had been feeling all of my life found some voice through her. Let me put it this way. I say this to my students all of the time. I don't think we really have very much to tell poems; I think poems have a great deal to tell us. That was the first poem that actually spoke *to* me, and I think that was a cornerstone and a beginning, like the poem itself could talk.

ELLIOTT: I find that poem so interesting for its blend of things that may seem positive or negative but all of them on the verge of that moment of heightened awareness when something is going to happen, but you don't know what. Did you write it as a prose poem?

HOWE: Yes.

ELLIOTT: Because the line endings work pretty nicely.

HOWE: Well, it's a prose poem with lineation, I should say, because it has been reprinted differently, and it has bothered me. It's a prose poem, but it is supposed to look like that, so I guess it's a poem in lines, actually. I did work on the breaks and where it broke, but I wanted it to read as prose. I guess I wanted it both ways.

ELLIOTT: I think it succeeds in both ways. I've never actually looked at the text when I've heard you read it, but when you leave a rather decisive pause, are you honoring the line breaks?

HOWE: Sometimes, most times . . . So much of reading is about an audience. Today I was reading to those boys from Keystone College whom I asked to move from the back row up to the front who may have had to go somewhere. Not just to them, but I was aware of them, and I was aware that one was restless, and one was listening, and another one was kind of half listening. It depends on who is in the audience and how it is going, because it really is a conversation, and I want them to pay attention. Most of the time the pause is with a line break; those long lines do break. Sometimes the intonation changes with the audience.

ELLIOTT: I happened to speak with both Sharon Olds and Robert Creeley relatively close in time about line breaks, and of course Creeley always honors them.

HOWE: Sharon doesn't.

ELLIOTT: No, she doesn't. She said she doesn't want people to pause at the end of a line. She wants them to move right on to the beginning of the next line. You seem to be more on the Creeley side.

HOWE: I love line and I love syntax, and I love the way they push against each other. I love Creeley's work. I love his lineation. His poems have the musculature of someone really thinking. It's not the product of thought; it is the thought itself. His poetry enacts the act of the mind moving through time. I love Sharon's work too. Her work so much feels like it is speech said urgently in one breath to someone. There are no pauses, hardly ever.

ELLIOTT: How much did you have to work at the music of poetry? Is it something that came really naturally to you? It is certainly important to your work.

HOWE: Poetry to me is oral; it really should be said out loud. Now this third book might not be. It might be something you'd want to read quietly to yourself, which is weird. But I grew up with the Bible, with all that parallelism and anaphora and the rhythms of the Old Testament and the New Testament, the sound of that Hebrew prosody. So it's that kind of music in most of the poems. And I also think it is my desire to have them be experiences that actually happen between the speaker and the hearer so that they happen in the air. That has been important to me.

ELLIOTT: Stanley Kunitz's blurb on *The Good Thief* refers to you as "a religious poet." Do you wear that label comfortably?

HOWE: I was horrified when I read that. Then I understood. I'm obsessed with the metaphysical, the spiritual dimensions of life as they present themselves in this world, so I understand what he means. "Religious" sort of scared me at first, but it's okay; I accept it now. I think a lot of women writing now are religious poets or spiritual poets.

Elliott: Who comes to mind?

Howe: Brenda Hillman, Jean Valentine, Jane Hirshfield, Jane Cooper . . . Jane Kenyon I think was a very spiritual poet. A lot of the women I read I think are concerned with that. Jorie Graham is a metaphysical poet. I love the metaphysical poets of the 17th century. I love Donne and Herbert. So I am more at ease with what Stanley wrote now than when I first saw it.

Elliott: In an article in *The American Poetry Review* by Ira Sadoff he was talking about dichotomies between a more traditional approach to poetry and post-modern, language-based poetry. One of the oppositions he developed was between organic unity and (to use a phrase from your poem, "Memorial") "post-modern brokenness." When I read that poem and its reference to Carolyn Forche and the obsolescence of the personal narrative, I wonder how to take it because I think of much of your poetry as being personal narrative. In that poem when the speaker says, "James doesn't understand," it sounds as if she feels drawn to brokenness because of feeling devastated by Billy's death.

Howe: I think it is ironic statement: "He doesn't understand that the personal narrative is obsolete." I love Carolyn and I admire her as a poet and as a person in the world, but that book threw me, *The Angel of History*. Our friend Billy had just died and I was reading *The Angel of History* and Carolyn does say the book is in a bunch of voices because the personal narrative is obsolete, or something. It was one of those weeks where I was gripped by despair, because I do argue with the personal narrative. I love stories. Stories have saved my life, and I also question stories even as I tell them. Organic unity in the old sense can't exist anymore since we blew up Hiroshima and Nagasaki and since we know we are no longer who we think we are. But something does remain. Was it Hopkins who said, "A taste of self'? I guess I still believe in the soul even if I don't believe in identity. So that particular poem was struggling with that, and Billy's death had shattered a narrative that had ended in some ways with his death, a good friend of ours. I guess what I'm worried about in the personal narrative poem is the self, the speaking self being made, even inadvertently, heroic—always, you know, the sensitive, heroic self. "Memorial" tries to undercut that by the speaker admitting to feeling anger with her friend because he carried the ashes or being annoyed with her man because he doesn't understand the personal narrative is obsolete. It was allowing a fragmentation into the work and allowing a voice to be speaking that may or may not know her own limitations that might be obvious to a reader. I think the danger of the personal narrative poem is that we're creating the self that is speaking. All too often we create a self we can live with.

ELLIOTT: One of the things I was interested in having you talk about is the difference between your two books. The second book is much more straightforwardly personal, autobiographical even. And the first book more often works through parable and persona. Was there a transforming moment that took you from the first book to the second book? Are you continuing with that approach, or are the poems you have said you are working on for the third book turning away from that?

HOWE: My brother John's living and dying changed my aesthetic entirely. That's solely responsible—my involvement and response to his living and dying with AIDS. I wanted after that to make an art that was transparent, that was accessible to people who don't usually read poetry, to my brothers and sisters—wonderful, intelligent, smart people who want to read poetry if only they know what to read. Regular people. And I wanted it to be the kind of talk that people talk in sick rooms, where it is very direct and very understated. I wanted to make movies without the photographer's thumb in the way. I wanted to get out of the way and let some of these things just unwind, so people could see in and have their own experience. It became very important to me to document some of the things that happened. Of course they are still transformed, but that became important to me. And then of course that influenced the whole rest of the book, deeply. I didn't want anything about that book to be obscure. The situation was difficult. I wanted it to have a simple surface, but to allow in the depths that of course occur every moment in ordinary life. So it was very hard, and getting started was very hard. There are no metaphors and there is no slant. That was the main reason that book changed.

Now I want never to write anything personal again. I'm struggling with it a lot. This new work is personal, but it's also deflected through

186

some other stories and voices. It's still so new it's hard to talk about, but I really don't want to tell any more biographical stories or use those stories as ways into experience. I don't know what happened. I really don't. It's still in the stages where I'm showing poems to readers and they go, "No. No. Yes. No. No." And I realize in the last two years I've been swimming around.

I wish I were a different type of writer, sometimes I do. When Johnny died I was walking with Stanley Kunitz in front of my apartment building in Cambridge. It was a few months after Johnny died and I was saying to Stanley, I feel as if something has me in its mouth and is chewing me. Everyone who has known grief knows this. I hadn't known it quite yet, but it is nothing new to everybody else who has known grief. I said I feel something has me in its mouth chewing me and there is nothing for me to do but be chewed, and Stanley said, "Yes, and you must wait to see who you'll be when it's done with you." Because I wanted to write right away, and I couldn't, and I had to wait to see who I was going to be after this experience sort of had me for a while. I feel that's what's happening now. I have to wait and keep writing, but wait to see what really wants to have a hold of me next and who I am and then to write the next real collection. I don't seem to be a poet who can just keep writing all of the time. I admire those people who can. Sharon, for instance. She just writes poems and poems and poems and poems. My friend Tony Hoagland, whose work I adore, who is one of my primary readers—he and I are sending each other a poem a week right now. And I keep sending him poems that I know are approaching what I want, but they're not there yet, and he's sending me poems that are done, done, done. But it doesn't matter; it takes what it takes.

ELLIOTT: Some of the poems about John make him into a source of (I'm not sure if this is the right word) spiritual wisdom. In "The Gate," where he says, "This is what you have been waiting for," and in the little anecdote you tell in the introduction to *In the Company of My Solitude* where he asks, "What's next for you?"—in both cases calling attention to the importance of the present moment—he sounds like a Zen master.

HOWE: Yeah, he does.

ELLIOTT: Did he come into that through his suffering from disease, or was he always inclined in that direction?

187

HOWE: Well, I wish he were here so you could ask him that question. John died so young, twenty-eight years old and sick for three years. Sober for five. He was always a wise, beautiful spirit. As a little child he wrote the most beautiful things. He really was a beautiful spirit, but also like the rest of us—human, addicted, reckless, in love with thanatos as much as eros for many years. When he got sober and realized he was ill, it was as if the clarity of his spirit could come to the fore. I'm sure you have known many people who became ill and died. We're all going to become ill and die one day. It seems to me whoever you are, you just become more of it as you die. It's interesting to watch people I've loved die. My father, who was a wonderful and difficult, difficult man, when he died was probably never as happy as in those last few weeks. It was as if his spirit could finally be itself without contending.

John really did become quite luminous and more in love. But he was always very loving, always very devoted. He actually used to say, "This is what you've been waiting for" before he got sick, no matter what was going on. I had this huge heartbreak, and he said, "Marie, this is what you have been waiting for. Stop looking forward to something. This is it." I think he became even more so when he was sick. If he were here, he would argue with me. Of course, like everybody who is sick and dying, he was worried and afraid, and he was upset, and he was everything else too. It's hard to describe the kind of simplicity he seemed to come to. He was in love with Joe, which is a very important thing. I mean one of the things John said to me, which in the last few years I've been trying to put into so many failed poems, sounds so corny. He looked at me one day and said, "This is not a tragedy. I am a happy man. When I'm asked if I could love, I can answer yes." And that was a great joy to him.

ELLIOTT: The poem "The Promise," which refers to Buddhism, makes it seem that he has an intuitive understanding of it.

HOWE: [Laughing.] He's been there; he's dead, right? John and I had that kind of relationship where we could look at each other across the room and get it. He looked back up at me and couldn't talk. It was like, "I wish I could tell you what I know, but I can't." That's another poem where the speaker doesn't know how silly she is, really.

ELLIOTT: What was the age difference between the two of you?

HOWE: Eleven years—he was the second youngest in our family of nine kids. John used to say we were intimates from a cradle. When he was a little boy, I used to write plays for my family and everybody would have a part. Johnny would help me. We would sit when he was a little kid and write songs everybody would have to sing at holidays and Christmas and birthdays. He would sit next to me as I handed these things out. The night before he'd help me get the lines and stuff. We always wrote them together. I can't even remember when it began. He was always there with me in the attic, the two of us writing these things. It's funny, I haven't really thought about that for a long time.

ELLIOTT: Did you ever think of your second book as aligning yourself with the so-called confessional poets?

HOWE: No. I've always thought that was a funny word—confessional. I grew up in the confessional and the idea you can go in and tell the story of your sins and be forgiven. It's a powerful one. I mean, was Sappho confessional? She told what it was like for her to miss somebody and be in love. Was Keats confessional? He sits outside his friend's house all day and listens to one bird and writes "Ode to a Nightingale" because he's so depressed. He comes right out and says it: I'm so depressed I want to go where that bird is and never come back. He makes a decision right in the middle of the poem: No, I won't do that; I'll write this poem instead! I know, of course, there are differences, but Catullus, Cavafy—these are confessional poets, poets who are talking about the circumstances of their lives, and their outcry comes from that. I guess I'm a little concerned about us using that word, because it seems to diminish an impulse into one thing. Robert Lowell, supposedly the first confessional guy of this century, or Sexton—I mean, you couldn't find two more different poets than Lowell and Sexton, and yet they are both confessional poets. Sylvia Plath is supposed to be confessional, but it is so difficult to understand those last poems.

I feel like I'm talking around your question, but it's something I'm interested in and worth dwelling on. Any story told for its own sake is not poetry, it seems to me. We all have stories to tell. It's the complexity of the human heart that I think is poetry's subject—the complexity of the human experience. I think the best poets writing today represent that complexity in the broadest, deepest sense. So there are poets who tell personal stories but honor that complexity—Yusef Komunyakaa, for example, being an African-American man in Vietnam who writes about being in Vietnam. It's complicated; it's not just one thing, like, "I was in Vietnam and it sucked." I feel very interested in the experimental poetry that is going on right now. My friend Brenda Hillman I think is a genius. I think her work is written from her soul, from her life and her concerns, and yet it also experiments with language, punctuation, interruption, and a lot of elements of postmodern language poetry, but there is still a self talking. So I think maybe when we say confessional we mean a poet who writes about one thing, beats one drum, and we are supposed to feel something for that poet that's different from what we feel for ourselves or other people.

ELLIOTT: I was interested in your saying you don't want to write personal poems anymore. Is one of the dangers having people confuse your poetry with your life? Once I heard someone say to Sharon Olds, "Tell me, how old are your son and daughter now?" And she said, "I have no son or daughter. Those are fictitious children."

HOWE: I understand what she means. For example, with that poem "Practicing," which talks about being in the seventh grade and kissing girls in the basement, *The New Yorker* legal department called up and said, "Are those girls identifiable?" I said, well, Linda's basement was like a boat and Gloria's father did have a bar downstairs with plush carpeting, but I didn't kiss those girls. So, yes, they're identifiable, because the poem has great, great details from my childhood, but that to me is the answer to the question of whether it is autobiographical. It's all constructed. I didn't kiss those two girls. They were my best friends when I was a kid. I kissed other girls, but how could you give up those gorgeous details with those basements, and it poured into the poems. They still made me change the names. But what comes together in a poem isn't true, and that is why I understand Sharon's response.

I remember a man, a very lonely man, coming up to me at the end of a reading and looking into my face and saying, "I feel as if I have looked down a corridor and seen into your soul." And I looked at him and said, "You haven't." You know, Here's the good news and the bad news: you haven't! I *made* something, and you and I could look at it together, but it's not *me*; you don't live with me; you're not intimate with me. You're not the man I live with or my friend. You will never know me in that way. I'm making something, like Joseph Cornell makes his boxes and everyone looks into them, but it's the box you look into; it's not the man or the woman. It's alchemy of language and memory and imagination and time and music and sounds that gets made, and that's different from "Here is what happened to me when I was ten." That poem is a good example. Linda's boat basement and Gloria's plush carpeting were there, but they weren't *there* there.

ELLIOTT: The order of the poems in the three sections of that book naturally flows chronologically from your childhood, to John's death, to events that happened after. Was that the order you wrote them in?

HOWE: No, the poems about Johnny came first, and the first and third sections were kind of written at the same time. At the very last second the day before the book was going to go to press, my old friend Lucie Brock-Broido called me up and said, "I just saw your manuscript at someone's house and I have to tell you I think the order is all wrong! Those poems about Johnny came first; they should be the first section, so I really think you should move it." And I said, "What? Oh, my God." So I halt the presses and think about it for days. Stanley ended up looking at the book for me and said, "Keep it the way it is." It was agony at the very last minute because I took Lucie's advice very seriously. It would have been back to the truth again, but the book itself made for another story that was its own—*one* story.

ELLIOTT: In the same way that your poetry has gone through these two phases at least, with the third to be announced, has your attitude toward language or the degree of faith you have in language been altered?

HOWE: That's a really good question. This week I have no faith in language. I must tell you I don't, but that's my own failing, not language's. I feel like it's the last outpost for us humans. I take it very seriously. I feel language has been utterly cut off by this culture and used in the service of consumerism and that poetry insists on the integrity of words, of *a* word. The confessional mode in poetry might be spent, but it's so interesting that the memoir keeps crashing and crashing on our shore more and more and more. Why do we want to hear these stories? Why do we want to know what was it like for you? What was it like for you? The language itself I feel is endangered more than it has ever been. To try to say what we mean, to try to make something beautiful and meaningful from language, feels to me like a profound political act still and a spiritual act. It's really what Madison Avenue and people who sell things are doing. I feel like poets and writers are the monks writing illuminated manuscripts, in the sense of trying to preserve the integrity of language, just to expand the possibilities for expression, because the culture is trying to push us into the same twenty words over and over again.

People now want the information fast and they want a certain kind of information that they can eat, essentially, instead of dwelling with mystery. Negative capability, Keats called it—to dwell with uncertainty without grasping after an easy solution. A poem often asks us to dwell there, and it's unbearable, especially if you have no practice, if you don't read or if you don't go off by yourself and sit alone for a while. Even those of us who write, we're often rushing around. So this dwelling, not fully comprehending something instantly, is very difficult. Anything that pushes us into the depths of our being is very hard to bear. I find it hard to bear. Sometimes I open a book that's so beautiful I have to shut it because it hurts me. I can't stand it. It's like, Oh no! Oh no! Oh no! This is going to drive me into my own heart. A day or two days later I'm saying, All right, and I just surrender to it: Do it to me. Go ahead. I want it. I don't want it. I want it. I don't want it. It's so hard to be brought to that place and then to close it again. Right along side of that, though, we also have to talk about what it is with all this resurgence in poetry, poetry slams, MTV, rappers. There is still something else going on. Now maybe it's something you and I would not prefer to go to every single night, but there is still language being used to tell the truth of somebody's existence that's happening among these guys. Maybe not in every single community but in the culture at large, young people are taking poetry into their bodies and putting it out in a new way that's their own. That's exciting to me. It really is, and its kind of anti-academy, anti-intellectual stance is exciting to me. I think it's great. And you need the whole spectrum—*The Inferno* and the kids who are at the Nuyorican Cafe tonight. We need the whole thing.

I think this is an interesting time. A lot of rivers are coming together in a big swirling eddy—the formalists, the rappers, the marginal peoples, confessional poetry, experimental poetry, women's experimental poetry, poetry that's postmodern, that's language based, that doesn't believe in the integrity of the self, poetry that insists on the integrity of the self. All of it belongs to the human race. We need it all. I feel very deeply that all of this is what keeps poetry alive as an art. In the contention and the argument, in all that, it's healthy and interesting. It's a bewildering time, a very difficult time, but I still feel that poetry is a medium for the human voice or outcry, for the human experience. It's deep and clear. I'm just so glad they're still doing it after all these years. It feels as if there is no public discourse that anyone can trust. The media is bought and sold. But there is still some kernel of integrity in the public discourse, and it's poetry for me. I have faith in it, even though you don't make any money. Anybody can walk away with it. You don't have to pay a lot of money for it; you can memorize it and put it right in your body. There's something very important about making something that is valueless to the people who would co-opt it and sell it, and therefore it's priceless and ineffable and belongs forever to humans who can handle it. I still have faith in that, in spite of everything else that's going on around us.

Notes

Howe, Marie. *The Good Thief*. New York: Persea, 1988.
_____. *What the Living Do*. New York: Norton, 1998.
Howe, Marie and Micheal Klein, Eds. *In the Company of My Solitude: American Writing from the AIDS Pandemic*. New York: Persea Books, 1995.

Acknowledgments

These conversations first appeared in the following publications:

"An Interview with W. S. Merwin." *Contemporary Literature* 29.1 (1988): 1-25. © 1988 by the Board of Regents of the University of Wisconsin System. Reprinted courtesy of the University of Wisconsin Press.

"'At Home in the Dark': An Interview with William Stafford." *Michigan Quarterly Review,* Spring 1991.

"'A Priest of the Imagination': A Conversation with William Stafford." *Friends Journal*, November 1991.

"Sharing Language: A Conversation with William Stafford." *Teaching English in the Two-Year College*, December 1991.

"An Interview with Robert Creeley." *Sagetrieb,* 10:1-2, Spring/Fall 1991.

"An Interview with Robert Morgan." *The Chattahoochee Review*, 13:2, Winter 1993.

"'Precarious Balances': A Conversation with Stephen Dunn." *Mid-American Review* 15:1-2, 1995.

"David Ray: Activist Poet." *Ergo*, July-August, 1995.

"'Home Keeps Getting Bigger': A Conversation with Naomi Shihab Nye." *Tampa Review,* no. 12, Spring 1996.

"'Finding a Distinctive Voice': A Conversation with Lucian Stryk, Part 1." *Modern Haiku* 27:1, Winter-Spring 1996.

"'Finding a Distinctive Voice': A Conversation with Lucian Stryk, Part 2." *Modern Haiku* 27:2, Summer 1996.

"'Praise Is a Generative Act': A Conversation with Pattiann Rogers." *Tampa Review* no. 18, Spring/Summer 1999.

"'The Complexity of the Human Heart': A Conversation with Marie Howe." *AGNI* (online edition), July 2004.

Some of these conversations were reprinted in whole or in part in the following publications:

"An Interview with Robert Creeley." Rpt. in *Contemporary Literary Criticism*. Ed. James P. Draper. Vol. 78. Detroit: Gale, 1994.

"Sharing language: A Conversation with William Stafford." Rpt. in William Stafford, *Crossing Unmarked Snow: Further Views on the Writer's Vocation*. Ed. Paul Merchant and Vincent Wixon, Ann Arbor: University of Michigan, 1998.

"'A Priest of the Imagination': A Conversation with William Stafford." Rpt. in *Every War Has Two Losers: William Stafford on Peace and War*, Ed. Kim Stafford, Minneapolis: Milkweed Editions, 2003.

"'Precarious Balances': A Conversation with Stephen Dunn." Rpt. in *Contemporary Literary Criticism.* Ed. Jeffrey W. Hunter. Vol. 206. Detroit: Gale, 2005.

"'The Complexity of the Human Heart': A Conversation with Marie Howe." Rpt. in *The Norton Introduction to Literature,* 10th edition. New York: W.W. Norton, 2010.

Some of these conversations reprint entire poems by the authors and the following rights and permissions were acquired and apply:

CPSIA information can be obtained
at www.ICGtesting.com
Printed in the USA
BVHW03s1931200718
522225BV00001B/5/P

9 781640 425019